"*Street Shadows* is a pleasure. It is a subtle piece of work, and hard to capture in a few words. It is an experiment in finding the point of equilibrium where the self can emerge as the dispassionate *and* compassionate interpreter of experience. Walker never fails to be honest where truth is needed and he never fails to be gracious where generosity is possible."—Marilynne Robinson, author of *Gilead* and *Home*

"What makes *Street Shadows* so riveting is that it shows the struggle between good faith and bad faith playing out within a single human heart. Always this inner wrestling, and there are no excuses in this brave book. It is a watershed—perhaps 'post-racial'—memoir because it lets us see a black man as Everyman, a man on his way in the world and uninterested in the consolations of blame."—Shelby Steele, author of *The Content of Our Character*

"[A] spectacular debut. . . . A funny, poignant, thoughtful and exceptionally well-written memoir that follows Walker from Chicago to Africa and locations across the U.S., each of which is crisply, authentically captured. While delivering a thorough, personal take on race relations, opportunity, and privilege, Walker hooks readers with his prose and honesty, without plying for sympathy or playing to readers' preconceptions."—*Publishers Weekly*

"A daring, evocative, and unflinchingly honest memoir by an extraordinary writer with an extraordinary story to tell. On the basis of this impressive literary debut, I predict that we'll be reading Jerald Walker for years to come."—Robert Atwan, series editor of *The Best American Essays*

"*Street Shadows* is a powerful memoir narrated through colorful and moving stories. The movement of the memoir traces the narrator's life through delinquency, drug use, family tensions, and family tragedies, and adds real emotional muscle to the voice."—James Alan McPherson, author of *Elbow Room*

"What a powerful read. From the very first sentence of this incredible journey with this young man, I felt as if I knew Jerald Walker, not just through his words but through his heart. This is a must-read for everyone who cares about the questions and the quest that being a human requires."—Nikki Giovanni, author of *Bicycles: Love Poems*

UNIVERSITY OF NEBRASKA PRESS • LINCOLN

To Susan—
Thank you for
your support—I'm
truly honored to _readby_
your book soon!
J Walker

A Memoir
of Race,
Rebellion, and
Redemption

STREET SHADOWS

JERALD WALKER

First Nebraska paperback printing: 2012

Published by arrangement with Bantam Books, an imprint of
The Random House Publishing Group, a division of Random
House, Inc.

Library of Congress Cataloging-in-Publication Data
Walker, Jerald.
Street shadows: a memoir of race, rebellion, and redemption /
Jerald Walker.
p. cm.
Originally published: New York: Bantam Books, c2010.
ISBN 978-0-8032-4095-7 (pbk.: alk. paper)
1. Walker, Jerald. 2. Racism—Illinois—Chicago. 3. Racism—
Africa. 4. African Americans—Illinois—Chicago. I. Title.
E185.93.12W35 2012
305.8009773'11—dc23 2011037202

Book design by Liz Cosgrove.

Street Shadows is a work of nonfiction. Some names and
identifying details have been changed.

To Brenda, for patience,
and Adrian and Dorian, for purpose

AUTHOR'S NOTE

This is a true story. The names of many of the persons mentioned, as well as some details and events surrounding them, have been modified in order to protect their privacy.

I published an excerpt of these events in which I stated that my brother Tim did not attend a birthday party, and subsequently I discovered a photograph of that party in which, staring into the camera, is Tim. I have made the change here. On other occasions when I discovered my memory to be in conflict with fact, I sided with the latter.

The Past—the dark unfathom'd retrospect!
The teeming gulf—the sleepers and the shadows!
The past—the infinite greatness of the past!
For what is the present after all but a growth out of the past?
(As a projectile form'd, impell'd, passing a certain line, still
    keeps on,
So the present, utterly form'd, impell'd by the past.)

—Walt Whitman, "Passage to India"

CONTENTS

STREET SHADOWS

PROLOGUE: GODS

When my twin brother and I were born in 1964 there were eight years left to live. Our apartment was already stockpiled with food, though it is still unclear to me for what purpose, since, according to the church to which we belonged, all followers of our faith would become gods at the sound of Gabriel's horn. That would also be the moment my parents would regain their eyesight, allowing them to see their six children for the first time. This alone, it seemed to me, would have been reason enough to die.

In 1968, four years before we were to receive our salvation, Martin Luther King Jr. received his. We lived on Chicago's West Side then; I remember sitting with my family in the living room after word spread of his assassination, watching our neighborhood burn on the evening news. The volume was on mute while my older sister Mary described the madness to our parents. When she spoke of the police's use of water hoses and how they fired guns into the rioting crowds, my father shook his head and said that Jesus couldn't return too soon.

And then in 1970, with the world's end so near and the prime rate so low, my parents decided that if they were ever going to own a home, they'd better do it now. They put an offer on a four-bedroom bungalow on the South Side, right in the heart of a middle-class white community, without fear of protest or assault, as if we were gods already.

My parents' decision to move among white people did not sit well with some of our relatives, especially Aunt Bernice. She cleaned whites' homes for a living and spoke frequently of their lack of hygiene, the fact that they didn't use soap, for instance, and that they soiled their sheets and ate food right off the floor. This was to be expected, Aunt Bernice insisted, from a people who had enslaved our ancestors and still enslaved us now; just look at the awful schools in our communities, and the drugs and crime, look at how they kill off our leaders like they killed off King. "And you want to go *live* with these folks?" she asked, shaking her head. "Don't be surprised if you wake some morning to a cross burning in your front yard."

But because the Prophet said there soon would be crosses burning in *everyone's* front yard, my parents did not add this to their list of concerns, not until January 1, 1972, had come and gone and the world was still here, they were still blind, we were still mortals, and there was a basement full of baked beans and creamed corn. And on top of that, there was a mortgage to be paid that they could barely afford. The last thing they needed was a cross-burning. Every once in a while they had us look outside to make sure none was there, and one morning, instead of a burning cross, we found a seven-year-old white boy named Ryan. He wanted to know if my twin brother Jimmy and I could come out to play.

We weren't supposed to socialize with people not of our faith, so Jimmy and I were surprised when my father said we could go. We followed Ryan across the street and into his backyard where later that summer Jimmy broke both of his arms, though the cause was not racial violence, as Aunt Bernice first suspected, or God's wrath, as my parents first suspected, but calcium deficiency. Ryan introduced us to several other white kids in the neighborhood, and within a short period of time I had tangible evidence that some of the things Aunt Bernice said about whites weren't true. I had seen soap in their houses. I had seen them eat from bowls and plates. And I had been enslaved only once, for a mere ten minutes, due to Ryan's gimpy bathroom door.

A few years later he was gone. The other kids were as well, their parents' experiment with integration at its end. Perhaps if they had remained, the roots of my aunt's racist narrative would not have taken hold in my subconscious, a narrative that would find ample nourishment from the blacks who moved into the community and hated white people as much as she did. Soon it would be hard to remember that Ryan and the other kids had been nice to us, and that they had not pushed Jimmy off the swings and broken his arms, as he sometimes said. The only opposing narrative, as I recall, was from Tommy, my oldest brother, who, at thirteen, was already laying roots of his own to support his future conservative views. Tommy never spoke against whites. He never complained of racism. He talked only of self-reliance and self-help. So we hated him too.

But the majority of my negative energy in those days was reserved for our church. I hated how different it made me feel from other kids. I hated, for example, that we worshipped on Saturday instead of Sunday. We couldn't celebrate Christmas or birthdays. We couldn't dress up for Halloween or go trick-or-treating. Easter was also off limits. Most of all I hated how joyfully our members spoke of the coming Armageddon, as if it were no more than the circus. They could have their eternal life and communion with God. I wanted clowns.

A PLACE LIKE THIS

*T*he winos were already there, four middle-aged men wrapped in the coats of giants. I took my place among them. I removed my cigarettes from my pants pocket and distributed them to the fingers trembling toward me. We smoked in silence while responsible people hurried past, heading toward the elevated train station or to the stores that lined this strip of 35th Street. It was my day off from responsibility, I had decided; I'd called in sick to my unit clerk job at the medical center. I wasn't sure I'd return. I wasn't sure of much of anything, only that I was out of coke and it was important to be drunk until I got some more.

The winos' radar clicked in and they moved toward the door seconds before it opened. The proprietor stepped back as we entered, saying good morning to some of us by name. He went behind the counter where three other men stood praising Michael Jordan's antics they'd seen on TV. All of the winos headed in that direction. They wanted Wild Irish Rose and Mad Dog, kept on the glass shelves above the register, but I had scrounged enough money for something better. Minutes later I emerged from the store with a pint of cognac and a forty-ounce of Olde English 800. A boy who couldn't have been more than fourteen joined me. He asked me to help him buy some liquor. I told him no. I told him he should be in school. He laughed and said *I* should be in school.

Years later I would think back to that incident and wonder if the boy even existed, if he were merely my subconscious urging me toward the path of salvation. But I couldn't comprehend that then, had no way to recognize any latent desire to be saved. All I knew was that at twenty-one my life was a mess and couldn't get any worse. But things can always get worse.

Sometime later that day I woke on my couch to a ringing phone. It was my friend Greg bearing good news: He'd started working at a dope house near 47th and King Drive and asked if I wanted credit. I told him I'd be there as soon as I found a ride. I called my ex-girlfriend Pam. *"Fool,"* she hissed, "do you know what the hell time it is?" I didn't but she told me; it was close to midnight. I promised to get her high. Give her thirty minutes, she responded, maybe a bit longer because of the storm. I moved close to my window and saw that it was snowing, a full-scale blizzard, in fact, weightless flakes swirling in all directions.

While I waited I straightened up a bit, stuffing empty liquor bottles and canned goods into a large garbage bag. For the first time in two days I showered and brushed my teeth. I still had a little of the cognac left but I was out of beer and decided we'd stop and get some more.

The dope house was only a few miles away. Ten minutes after picking me up, Pam double-parked on a side street and let me out. Six inches of powder had blanketed the abandoned lot I trudged through, transforming the debris into something beautiful. When I reached the alley, I made a left and headed for the back stairs of a three-story brownstone. I was on the first landing when from behind me a man's voice ordered me to stop. Seconds later a hand rummaged through my coat pockets while another struggled to steady a gun. It vibrated against my temple.

"Where's the money?" the man demanded.

"I . . . I . . . don't have any."

"Don't *bullshit* me!"

I told the robber I wasn't bullshitting him, that I was only there to see a friend. He pulled four envelopes from my back pocket, the mail I had grabbed before leaving my apartment lobby. He stuffed them inside his coat and backed away. I turned to leave.

"No, no." He motioned the gun up the stairs. "Go where you were going."

I went to the third floor. At apartment six I slipped a hand through the burglar bars to knock on the door. It opened before I touched it, just wide enough for me to see a sliver of Greg's dark brown face and his signature tan beret.

"I was just robbed," I said.

"What?"

"Right downstairs!"

We both laughed and shook our heads. "You're the second one today," he responded, handing me a gram of coke between the rusted wrought iron. For my "inconvenience" he gave me another one at half price. I promised I'd pay him in two days.

Back at the car, I told Pam about the gunman.

"He didn't get the coke, did he?" she asked.

"No," I told her, "he robbed me as I was going up the stairs. He was gone when I came down."

"You a lucky motherfucker," she said. " 'Cause I'd have killed you for having me come out here for nothing."

She knew what mattered.

"Let's get some beer," I suggested.

Thirty minutes later we were back at my apartment, and sometimes I imagine that as the first line of coke entered my body, the first bullet entered Greg's. I see our heads tilting back simultaneously, mine coming to rest on my vinyl couch, Greg's on the snow-covered tenement stairs. I reach for Pam to rub her thigh as the gunman reaches for Greg to search his pockets. Pam rises and moves toward the bathroom, pausing to wink at me, and the gunman rises to run into the shadows, pausing to shoot Greg five more times. Greg is found with a .32 still in his hand, unused, and

Pam finds me with a can of beer in mine, unopened. Greg is dead. Pam is naked. I believe myself to be a lucky man.

I know I am a minute later when I hear the news.

My older brother Tim called to deliver it. He'd arrived on the scene shortly after me in search of free dope too, but instead found a crowd of nighthawks contemplating a corpse, everyone hoping, no doubt, that it wasn't someone they knew. At first no one could tell; part of his face was missing. But a tan beret was there.

"Maybe . . . ," I stammered, "maybe somebody else had the same beret . . ."

"Naw, it was his. He's *dead*."

I denied it. Tim insisted and I denied it some more until I did so in quivers, then whispers, and when I fell silent he said he had to go.

I set the phone back on the receiver. Pam tried to comfort me, her hand light on my shoulder. I pushed it away. I told her to get her things and leave. I was slumped on the couch, naked but for my briefs and socks, my bowed head between my hands, half seeing Pam throw on her clothes, half hearing her curse me.

Before she was out the door I'd started crying, wailing like a baby, and even then I knew the life I grieved was my own. Where was the elementary school bookworm? Where was the high school honor student? What had happened to my love of reading? I was a drug addict, high at that very moment on the coke of a dead friend.

I cried until I couldn't cry anymore and then I rose with the plate of coke and paced the room. I stopped at the window. Outside the snow fell steadily, making its haphazard descent to the street sixteen floors below, and I imagined how it would scatter in my wake as I tumbled through it. This vision replayed in my head as I snorted another line. Then I opened the window. Rather than cold air rushing in, I could feel the warm air rushing out, coaxing me, showing me the way. Several minutes passed before I extended the plate over the sill.

Twenty-five years later, tossing the drug to the wind is still the second most difficult thing I've ever done. The most difficult thing is still that I didn't follow it.

But in a way I did. I withdrew from everyone, so thoroughly isolating myself that the body at Greg's funeral might as well have been my own. I refused all social invitations. I accepted no visitors. I wouldn't even speak to Tim.

I left my apartment only to go to work and to the grocery store. For six months my sole companions were telemarketers, smooth-talking men who stayed up with me all night giving counsel, telling me how to get my life together. I was assured from the deck of a yacht that I could make a million dollars selling real estate. I was told that I could regain vigor with the purchase of a juicer. Ginsu knives, I was promised, could make me happy.

Sometimes I received counseling from a porn star. She wore red lingerie as she lay on a bed next to a telephone and behind a stuffed bear that she gently stroked. If I was lonely, she said, I needed simply to pick up the phone and call. One night I did. "What's your name?" she moaned. I started telling her, not realizing she was a recording until she interrupted me, not understanding that I was paying good money only to listen. But I wanted to talk, too. I hung up and called someone else.

"I'm an alcoholic," I said.

The woman who'd answered the hotline already knew. "Yes, yes," she replied. "Of course you are." Her voice was soothing and kind; I got the sense she cared about me. She asked me what prompted me to call.

"Your commercial," I told her.

Now she wanted to know my drinking habits, examples of how liquor was affecting my life. I told her it made me do things I'd probably never do while sober, such as make this call.

"Have you been drinking?"

"Yes." And then I added, "But only beer." It was all I allowed myself, less and less as the weeks went by.

"People often call while drinking," she told me. She wanted me to come to a meeting. I said I would. She took my zip code and gave me the address of a substance abuse center not far from where I lived. "So, you'll be there Saturday at nine, Mr. Jenkins?"

Bobby Jenkins was the name I'd given her. "Sure," I said, "I'll be there Saturday."

But I did not go.

I did not go to the AIDS meeting either.

"Don't die alone," that counselor had pleaded with me, a passionate man who seemed close to sobbing. "We can *help* you. You must want help," he reasoned, "or you wouldn't have called."

"True," I said.

"How long have you been infected?"

"I'm not sure that I am."

"Have . . . have you been tested?"

"No."

"Have you had unprotected sex with an infected partner?"

"No."

"Are you an intravenous drug user?"

"No," I said.

He hung up.

I bought a Bible. I read from it every morning from four to five o'clock with a televangelist who spoke calmly and reasonably from behind a desk. I ordered the book he'd written, which contained the ten keys to life and the afterlife, five keys on each side. During the month or so he counseled me, the childhood memories of going to church every week with my family made me unbearably nostalgic. After one of my sessions with the reverend, I called home. My mother answered; it was the first time I'd heard her voice in two years. She didn't seem to mind that it wasn't yet dawn. "I think I'd like to go to church with you and Daddy this

Saturday," I said. But they had stopped going. I was shocked by this news, because they had always been strict believers, or maybe, it occurred to me, they'd only been strict church attendees. It was just as well, though, because I didn't really want to go back to church. I wanted to go back in time.

I kept calling my parents, sometimes several times a week. I decided to contact my two sisters as well, both of whom had been horrified by the lifestyle I'd chosen seven years earlier. They were surprised to hear from me, even more surprised when I invited them to my apartment for dinner. Next I invited my brother Tommy to watch a Bears game. During each of these gatherings, my brother and sisters counseled me, too, just like the telemarketers, and I listened with an opened mind about the armed services, the field of computer repair, the money to be made as a stockbroker.

Someone mentioned yoga, and I was immediately attracted to what it promised—spirituality without God, sanctity without religion. A stress-free existence. I found a yoga instructor in the Yellow Pages. The woman who answered the phone mentioned some of the masters she'd learned from, people with multisyllabic names that began with the letter *K*. There was a class the next morning, she told me, if I was interested. I said I was. She told me to wear comfortable clothing and that payment—fifty dollars for the first three sessions—should be in cash. Before we hung up, she asked me my name. "Jenkins," I said. "Bobby Jenkins."

At nine the next morning I wandered around the neighborhood of Hyde Park, feeling half tourist, half prowler among the million-dollar homes. I'd been to Hyde Park before—a friend had moved to the area with his family when we were teens—but never to this part of town. This was near the University of Chicago, and as I continued walking, some of the campus's majestic Gothic buildings came into view, looking not unlike the Emerald City. People my age rode toward the campus on bicycles, or marched on foot hauling large backpacks. It was autumn, the start of the semester I could only assume because I knew nothing about college. I continued looking for my yogi.

I found her house at last, a three-story Queen Anne with a bright yellow door. I rapped the lion-headed knocker five quick times. A man probably in his twenties answered. He wore a long beard and his hair was twisted in a white version of dreadlocks, the ends held together by colorful rubber bands. "I'm looking for"—I glanced down at the paper in my hand—"Ms. Friend."

"Sure," he said. "Follow me." I noticed a vague hint of marijuana in the air as I was led through the parlor to a narrow flight of stairs. The surrounding walls were covered in rich burgundy wallpaper that I couldn't resist touching. It felt like crushed velvet, some of it worn thin from a century's trace of curious hands. At the landing we made a right and passed several closed doors, finally stopping at the end of the hall near a pedestal holding a hookah. The man stepped to the side and motioned toward a room on his right. The door was slightly ajar. I opened it and walked inside.

It was bare except for a mat in the center of the floor, pictures on the wall of elderly dark-skinned men in loincloths, and, in a chair by a window, a morbidly obese woman. I turned to look at the man who'd escorted me but he was gone. I looked back at the woman. She furrowed her brow and glanced upward as her arms slowly rose from her sides, Moses in a white muumuu before the Red Sea. "Please remove your shoes, Mr. Jenkins," she said, "and let us begin."

For the next hour she talked me through a number of poses, telling me their names and explaining what they would do to improve my flexibility and worldview. She never left her chair. And I never left her instruction. I would wonder about that for a long time afterward, concluding only that nearly a decade of drug and alcohol abuse had so destroyed my self-esteem that learning yoga from an overweight woman in a chair did not anger me. But I did have enough self-esteem left to know, even as I was paying her the fifty dollars, that I would not return for the next two sessions. I walked away from her house feeling duped and as confused about what to do with my life as ever.

The next six months brought no more clarity. But they did bring books. I'd joined the Book of the Month Club and now my companions were the authors who regularly arrived at my door. I read constantly and indiscriminately, sometimes all through the night and always on the trains going to and from the medical center. And I read there, too, since I worked the second shift, 3:00 PM to midnight, and there was never much to do. I generally kept to myself, but suddenly I was an object of attention and curiosity; not many unit clerks spent their downtime reading, and if they did it was *The National Enquirer* rather than *Mayday: Eisenhower, Khrushchev and the U-2 Affair.* There seemed to be a consensus among my colleagues that I should be in school.

I deflected questions about college by saying I couldn't afford it or that I was saving money in order to go. But the truth was that the thought of going terrified me, not because I might fail, but because I might succeed. I had made a life for myself within the urban underclass, and even though that life was filled with boundaries and constraints, there was a certain comfort there. There was no comfort in allowing myself to be free.

But now comfort of any sort was increasingly hard to find. I hated my job. I hated the thought of always having it. And I hated myself when the train I rode to and from work pulled into the Halsted Street station, home of the University of Illinois at Chicago. Twice a day I would look up from a book and watch people of all ages enter and exit the double doors with backpacks bearing the school's logo. I would glance over the expressway toward the university's buildings, sometimes imagining myself in one of them taking a class. I did this without fail until at last, when the vision of myself as a college student no longer struck me as absurd, I stood when the students around me stood, and moved with them toward the double doors. I half expected someone to stop me.

We exited the train and walked as a group up the platform stairs before turning right and heading for the campus. The traffic light in front of us flashed from green to yellow; I found myself sprinting with the others to make it across the street in time. It was there that the group—maybe twenty of us—began to disperse. I picked someone to follow, a woman in a red parka. She led me straight to the library, an imposing concrete structure with narrow windows. I hesitated before entering, but only for a second. The woman in the parka stopped at the circulation desk. I found a seat at an empty table and opened my book. For the few minutes I sat there pretending to read, I feared that at any moment someone would spot me and instantly know that I was not one of them, that I did not belong. I stayed only ten minutes before my paranoia forced me to leave.

I went back the next day and, emboldened by the previous day's success, stayed for a full hour. I went twice more the following week. And then going to the campus became my morning routine. One day I stopped at the campus store, bought a backpack with the school logo, and filled it with my accumulated book club selections. I ate lunch in the cafeteria. I bought a sweatshirt that said UIC FLAMES and wore it while I sat in the library pretending to study. For two months I was an impostor, an infiltrator in a forbidden land, until I managed to convince myself that this land was mine, as much my right as any other's. An admissions counselor disagreed.

"You'll *never* be accepted here," he told me. I was in his office, or rather at his desk in a large room full of other desks, counselors, and prospective students. He'd just finished reviewing my application, having lowered it from his puzzled face to confirm with me that I was indeed twenty-two years old, had received failing grades in high school, and had dropped out at age sixteen. While he slowly shook his head, I glanced around the room. Young people were everywhere, smiles on some of their faces, their futures spread before them like red carpets. I looked back at the counselor. He handed me my application. When he apologized and wished me well, there was genuine pity in his voice, just as there had been in the voices of my high school teachers and my parents when they saw me going down, caught in the urban undertow. And now I smiled because I knew there was no need to be pitied anymore. I had resurfaced, after all. I had survived. I had a backpack full of books. I had toured a college campus and even read in its library. And I knew that, somewhere, there had to be a place like this for a person like me.

SCHOOLED

*W*hen my brother Tim was eigh-teen, he received a scholarship to study mathematics at the Illinois Institute of Technology. Two years after he started classes, when I was fourteen, he tried to lure me into his world of probabilities and figures, taking me with him to hear lectures on Ptolemy's theorem and Benford's law. But it didn't stick; I was a poet at heart, too quick to laugh and cry, too slow to rationalize and reason. I spent my free time devouring novels, anything I could get my hands on, including my sister Linda's Harlequin Romances. Tim snatched one out of my hands one day and rapped it against my head. "Those are for sissies," he said.

Sissies was not a word the Walkers used. If my parents had heard him he would have been sternly punished. "Here," he con-tinued, tossing me a paperback. "Read this." It was *Pimp: The Story of My Life* by Iceberg Slim. I cracked it open and scanned the first paragraph:

> Her name was Maude and she "Georgied" me around 1921. I was three years old. Mama told me about it, and always when she did her rage and indignation would be as strong and as emotional perhaps as at the time when she had sur-prised her panting and moaning at the point of orgasm

with my tiny head wedged between her ebony thighs, her massive hands viselike around my head.

I looked up. Tim winked at me as he turned to leave. I lowered my gaze back to the page and didn't lift it again until the book was finished. The lives it had rendered were terrifying and sinful, different in every way from mine and the people I knew. I hadn't really even understood much of what I'd read. But I was curious, and that mattered more.

A few days later, Tim told me it was time.

"For what?" I asked.

He said, "To be schooled." He led me to our parents' garage, where my twin brother was leaning against the hood of the family station wagon, a beer in one hand, a joint in the other. I was astonished, especially when I learned that Tim had been getting him high for months. "I wasn't ready for you yet," Tim said. "I wasn't sure if I should let you turn out like Tommy." They both laughed. Our brother Tommy was twenty-one and still as straitlaced as the pope. I had not been entirely opposed to turning out like Tommy, but I was very much opposed to being laughed at. I opened a beer and took a swallow.

"Want to try some weed?" Jimmy asked.

"Sure," I said. He handed me the joint. I took a hit, triggering a bout of choking from me and hysterics from my brothers.

"You all right?" Tim asked, patting me on the back. "You okay?"

When I could speak, I said, "Hell yeah." I'd never cursed before. "*Hell* yeah," I said again. After the joint was gone, we grabbed the rest of the beers and headed inside, settling in the living room in front of the TV.

It was still early in the evening, probably around seven. Other than our recently adopted two-year-old brother André, whom I assumed was sleeping because I didn't see or hear him, none of our siblings was home. Our parents were in their bedroom next door, but since they were blind it didn't matter. Tim only had to whisper when he schooled me. "The Prophet is nothing but a hustler," he said, "and we've all been his marks."

I'd learned the meaning of "marks" from Iceberg Slim. I'd learned "tricks" and "johns" too, which Tim also said we were. "How do you know this?" I asked.

Tim grinned. "Let's just say it's been *revealed* to me," he said, sounding very much like a prophet himself. But in 1978, you didn't have to be a prophet to know that the world had not ended in 1972, nor later, in 1975, the Prophet's revised time of peril. I remembered how, on the eve of 1975, I lay in bed unable to sleep, waiting for the stroke of midnight to arrive, when God would swing his mighty arm through the clouds and knock the unchosen from the earth, like chess pieces. As soon as my clock read eleven fifty-five, I tiptoed through the house and stood in front of my parents' bedroom door. When their vision was restored, I wanted to be the first person they saw.

"Everything about the church," Tim continued, "all that stuff we were raised believing, *were lies*." A chilling bitterness crept into his voice when he began speaking of the secret extravagant lifestyle the Prophet lived by pilfering church funds, a charge that would also be leveled by the investigative reporter Mike Wallace a few months later on *60 Minutes*. I looked at Jimmy for his reaction to this disturbing news, but he'd nodded off in the easy chair. I looked back at Tim. He was staring intently at the TV, which I understood to mean, at least for the moment, that my schooling was done.

SEDUCED

A tall white male walked into the classroom with papers in one hand and an unlit cigarette in the other. He wore typical professor attire—wrinkled khakis, oxford shirt, and tweed blazer—and his hair was gray and flourishing on the sides and in back, enough to comb some of it over a bald spot and to have a ponytail. He sat at his desk, put on a pair of half-rimmed glasses, and began reading names from a list, pausing to look up when someone responded. A dozen students sat before him, most of us black, most of us in our twenties, and all of us academically unfit to be anywhere but there.

I sat in the back row, hoping to go unnoticed as I continued to test the academic waters, tests that so far hadn't gone very well. I had already failed three classes. They had not been difficult; I'd simply stopped attending after deciding my life's calling was not architecture or sociology, but rather political cartooning. So I enrolled in a private art school only to discover I could neither afford the tuition nor draw. And now I was back here again, at Loop Community College, bobbing along the curriculum like driftwood. On a whim, I'd signed up for a course in creative writing.

The professor called my name. I raised my hand. He raised his eyebrows. "My dear boy," he said. "Why *on earth* are you so far away?" Before I could think of a response he lit his cigarette, exhaling the smoke toward a NO SMOKING sign. He pointed toward an empty desk in the front row. "Come, come. Deposit yourself right here." As I reluctantly stood, all of the students stared at me and a few of them snickered. I ballooned with embarrassment and considered walking right out the door; only the thought of further humiliation prevented me. But by the time I took my seat, I'd decided to drop the class the next morning. "Much better," he continued. "After all," he added, "what's the point of being a rebel if no one can see you rebelling?"

"Who said I was a rebel?" I asked.

"You did," he replied, "and that's the power of the objective correlative, one of a writer's most important tools. Now, class, imagine this: The story you're reading opens to a young man sitting along the back wall of his class, with not one but *two* empty rows in front of him. He's wearing a black leather biker's jacket, black pants and shirt, combat boots, and sporting a mustache that curves *ever so slightly* down the edge of the lips in the perfect mimic of his *ever so slight* frown. His arms are folded across his chest, and his long, thin legs, stretched into the aisle, are crossed at the ankles. The writer of this story is very skilled, for he has had the protagonist say not one word, *not one word,* and yet the protagonist has told us he is a rebel, he is a loner, he is iconoclastic, and—most important—he is *hiding* something." The professor looked at me and smiled with teeth too perfect to be real. "Now, we don't yet know what he is hiding, do we? For that, we must read the entire story."

But he'd already read my entire story, even the parts still unknown to me. "You'll go far," he'd soon be telling me, and I would want desperately to see what he saw, this future place where my life turned out well. At the moment, though, all I could see was what was behind me, a wasteland of failures and defeats.

We first shared our respective visions with each other a month into the semester.

He'd taken me to lunch, a fast-food restaurant near the school.

As soon as we carried our baskets of hot dogs and fries to the table, he—Edward Homewood—asked me how old I was.

"Twenty-four," I said.

"How old were you when you dropped out of high school?"

I squinted at him, curious how he knew. I wondered if he'd checked the school's records, or if I'd been exposed by my poor grammar. "Sixteen," I told him, unwilling to say more.

He said it for me. "You were bored shitless with your classes, no doubt, and the streets were more alluring."

I nodded.

He took a bite of his hot dog. "Tell me more."

I confessed some of my crimes, literally, starting with the burglary of my high school that accelerated my downward spiral. I told him of other burglaries, of other thefts. I mentioned my addictions and arrests, the violent death of a close friend, the murder conviction of another—laying before him a few of the things he'd told the class I was hiding.

He swept them away. "We've all sinned," he said.

I mentioned one more thing, a bag of groceries I took from an elderly lady, expecting and wanting a moral stoning. Instead, he threw confetti. "What *wonderful* material you have," he said, beaming. And then he praised the stories I'd written so far, tales of urban mayhem so autobiographical that as I'd typed them, and even as he cited them now, I cringed with remorse and guilt.

"So," he asked, "what's your major?"

I hunched my shoulders, waiting for him to tell me.

"English," he declared, and then he mentioned the Iowa Writers' Workshop, which I'd never heard of. Nor had I heard of its famous alumni, bestselling and prizewinning authors whose names he pulled from the smoky air. I'd never considered being a writer, but his belief that I could both intrigued and confused me. *He* intrigued and confused me. Especially when he reached out to touch my hand, patting his fingers lightly against mine. I didn't know what to make of that.

My girlfriend Erica did. "He's trying to get into your pants," she said when I told her. "What do you think all that flattery is for?"

I reminded her that she liked my writing too.

"It's my job to be supportive. I'm your girlfriend."

"He's my professor."

"He's your *gay* professor who *touched* you."

But the act of writing had touched me as well. Since the first class assignment, I'd been doing it every day, cranking out stories and essays as quickly as I could type them. Each one that failed hit me hard; the successes made me high. But I'd sober up quickly and go at it again.

And to think of how many drugs I'd used, so much deadly experimentation, when this, all along, was what I'd been searching for.

I now realized I'd been searching for Professor Homewood too, a teacher who would tell me, as so many other teachers had before him, that I would go far. I didn't care if he said it while his hand was on mine. And I didn't care that many of the books he gave me had homosexual themes. Some of them were so ancient that mold had eaten away the edges, but usually they were brand-new hardbacks, the receipts wedged between uncracked spines. He never wanted them back, and soon they began to cover my desk at home, a monument, Erica insisted, to his true intentions. But I chose to see the books as merely a way to broaden my horizon, Professor Homewood's attempt to offer me a glimpse into his culture.

"So why is he always hugging on you?" Erica asked when I offered this explanation. They'd met a few times by then at college functions. "I mean, what's that all about?"

"Don't start."

"I'm just saying."

"He's affectionate. So what?"

She shrugged. "I'm just saying."

I went back to my book. Erica took it from me and read the title. *"The God of Ecstasy: Sex Roles and the Madness of Dionysos."* She tossed it onto my lap and left the room.

A month later, I decided not to tell her when he touched my knee. "As soon as I finished reading your first story," he was saying at the time, "I thought I must get this boy to Iowa City." So far he had only gotten me to his couch. It was my first time at his condo, a plant- and book-cluttered two-bedroom unit on Chicago's North Shore. He patted my knee and I thought of Erica's warning that he'd ply me with liquor and try to seduce me. I'd just finished my third glass of scotch. He reached for the bottle and poured me more.

We drank for another hour, talking about my stories, the classics he wanted me to study, writing exercises I should do. He laid out a two-year plan of courses for me to take at Loop College and told me the names of teachers to seek or to avoid. By 1:00 AM, when I rose to leave, my academic path to Iowa City had been charted. As we stood at his door, he ignored my attempt to shake his hand and hugged me. His lips pressed against my check, and I noted the peculiar sensation of stubble brushing stubble. I turned and, more than a little tipsy, staggered a few steps down the hall, stopping at the elevator whose doors were already opened. Before entering them, I turned around.

"Professor Homewood?"

"Yes?"

"Do you really think I can make it?"

"Yes," he said. "I do."

"Are you sure?"

"Unequivocally," he said. "Aren't you?"

I nodded.

As I made my way home, I thought of the teachers at my high school who had tried to elicit that response from me, and I wondered how different my life would have turned out if I could have given it. And I remembered how opposed I'd been to attending the elite college preparatory school my elementary teachers had urged me to, how I'd pleaded with my parents not to make me go. Fear of opportunity is a terrible thing. But regret is worse.

"I'm leaving," I told Erica when I got home. "I'm moving to Iowa City to finish my degree in two years." I'd been considering the idea for a while, since Professor Homewood had raised the possibility, but this was my first mention of it. Perhaps that moment was not the best. I was on my knees on the bathroom floor, having just emptied my stomach in the toilet. Erica helped me to my feet. We walked to the bedroom in silence. I collapsed onto the mattress, still clothed. She stood at the foot of the bed now, untying one of my shoes. "Come with me," I said. We'd been together for two years by then, since 1987. We'd lived together for one. There'd been talk of marriage and children. But she had a good job as a nurse and was about to start graduate school. All of her family was in the area. "Will you come?" I asked. She still didn't respond. But when she folded her arms across her chest and looked away, I had my answer. The power of the objective correlative.

We had been driving for only four hours, but the cornstalks we passed might as well have risen from a field in Rome. I stared out the passenger window, dumbfounded by the expanse of earth, the vastness of the horizon, and for the first time realized how small my life had been. I could feel myself shrinking.

A short while later the size of the campus, innumerable buildings scattered over acres and acres of land, shrank me some more. An hour into the tour, Professor Homewood parked the car and we traversed the center of town on foot, browsing through the public library, resting on benches while children splashed in a fountain nearby, eating a late lunch in my first Thai restaurant. We stopped at a bookstore called Prairie Lights where he bought me a copy of Bruce Chatwin's *Songlines,* writing inside the front cover, "On the occasion of the first visit to the heartlands, Iowa

City, 1990." Then we went to the Writers' Workshop office. It was late in the afternoon on a Friday, and only the secretary, Deb West, was still there. That didn't matter. Professor Homewood, standing behind me, his hands on my shoulders, marched me forward until my thighs pressed against her desk. *"This,"* he said, "is Jerry Walker. He'll be transferring here in a few months to complete his undergraduate degree. After that, he'll be applying to the Workshop." Awkward smiles all around.

And then a quick stop at the admissions office, where I picked up a transfer application and a stack of brochures. Next we went to the campus bookstore. Professor Homewood headed straight to a display table covered with a mound of sweatshirts. He held one up in front of me, nodded approvingly at the Hawkeye mascot, and then tucked it under his arm as we got in line.

In the car he asked, "So, what do you think of it all?"

"It's okay," I said, not wanting to sound too excited. "Yes, I can definitely see myself here."

It was dark by then, the sun having recently set in the early-August sky. We were headed to spend the night at the house of his friend, a woman he'd attended The University of Iowa with in the 1950s. I turned on the light above me so I could look at the brochures, marveling at all the course offerings, the endless extracurricular activities, the sports teams, and then coming to a halt when I reached the out-of-state tuition. I ran the enormous numbers over in my head, moving them around, squeezing them, trying to make them shrink along with me. They wouldn't. Behind me, my dream receded with the campus.

I must have sighed or cursed; Professor Homewood asked me what was wrong. "Tuition's pretty steep," I mumbled, not expecting that he would offer to help me pay it. I was speechless when he did. And yet, somehow, I was also not surprised. For the rest of the ride, I sat quietly thinking of all that he had done for me, wondering how I could ever repay him.

By the time we reached his friend's house, we were in a celebratory mood. We sat in her country-style kitchen drinking heavily until 2:00 AM. When ten seconds couldn't pass without someone yawning, we knew it was time to turn in. Professor Homewood and I grabbed the bags that we'd parked by the door and followed our hostess up the stairs of her two-story bungalow. She pointed out the bathroom as we passed it before gesturing to an open door on her left. Wishing us good night, she headed back the way we had come.

Professor Homewood and I started to walk into the room, but I stopped when I saw what was before me—one bed. For an instant, my old fear and self-doubt manifested itself in a single terrible thought: Erica had been right all along. Getting me interested in writing, constantly praising my academic abilities, was just a part of Professor Homewood's elaborate ploy to lead me to this city, to this room, to this bed. I didn't have what it took to be at a major university. I'd never be a writer.

"Perhaps one of us should sleep on the couch," he said.

I was still standing by the door, I realized, my mouth open. Professor Homewood had realized it too. He looked wounded, like a man falsely accused of lying. I walked in and sat my backpack near one of the pillows. "That's not necessary," I said.

"I don't mind taking the couch."

"This is fine."

"Are you sure?" he asked.

I said, "Unequivocally."

We exchanged smiles. He carried his bag to the bathroom. I undressed and put on my pajamas. A moment later he returned wearing something out of Dickens, a long white nightgown that fell to his ankles, and a matching nightcap. I went to brush my teeth. His teeth, I saw, were in a cup of blue liquid on the vanity. When I returned to the room, he was already in bed, thumbing through one of the brochures, but he placed it and his glasses on the nightstand when he saw me. I turned off the light switch by the door and then lay next to him. A brief conversation about a book he was reading ended midsentence when, after a short silence, his snore filled the room. I closed my eyes, but I could not sleep. I lay there imagining myself still on the university's campus, and then I thought of Professor Homewood, and all of my teachers before him, who had finally gotten me there.

THE LAKE OF FIRE

*T*im drove my fourteen-year-old twin and me around the block with the windows down and the heater blasting to help get rid of the smell of marijuana. When Tim, Jimmy, and I pulled up in front of our house, our parents were coming down the porch steps with our baby brother, André, and our oldest brother, Tommy, but only one of our sisters, Linda, because Mary was away at college. After they piled in with us, we headed off to church.

We were greeted at the door by Mr. Paulson, our middle-aged minister whose short Afro stood in defiance of a big-Afro world. We didn't make fun of him, though, because he was already an object of pity; it was rumored that his ten-year-old daughter had lost her mind as soon as she learned that she and her mother were being forced to leave town.

The Prophet would say that the children's mental instability was due to their mixed blood. God strictly forbade interracial marriage because, according to the Prophet, himself a white male, it weakened the superior white race and it did the inferior ones no favors. He preached that we should marry our own kind, even within our own kind: redheads should marry redheads, light-skinned blacks should marry light-skinned blacks, midgets should marry midgets. And people of mixed race should of course marry each other, thereby making the best of a bad situation.

If Mr. Paulson and his white wife had researched the doctrine of the church, they might not have been so interested in joining. That was probably true of most of the people who, like my parents, had been sucked into the whirlwind of the Prophet's charisma, which Mr. and Mrs. Paulson first experienced one Saturday morning as they sat listening to their radio. They noted the frequency of the station, as well as the time of day, and then they tuned in regularly for two months until there was no doubt in their minds that this was the word of God. After contacting the church and inquiring about joining, they were interviewed by three deacons who were sent to their home. The deacons congratulated the Paulsons for being chosen, gave them brochures, reviewed the church's overall philosophy, prayed with them, read scriptures with them, and then explained that, unless they separated soon, the entire family would burn in the lake of fire.

She took the daughter. He took the son. Now heaven, they were promised, would take them all.

After he became a minister, the lake of fire became Mr. Paulson's signature theme, slipped in at least once during each of his sermons, as it was that morning I sat there stoned. I tried to ignore his vivid description of my fate by drawing pictures on my notepad and handing them to my seventeen-year-old sister. The latest one was of a robot that I'd surrounded with musical notes. Linda wrote "Dancing Machine" beneath it before handing it back. I drew another one, this time of Bozo crying. "Tears of a Clown," Linda wrote. As I tried to think of something more difficult to draw, I heard the minister boom, *"And he who hath not been redeemed shall burn in the lake of fire!"* I closed my eyes and promised God I'd never get high again.

After church we climbed back into our station wagon and headed home. Once there, we spent the next several hours sitting around waiting for the Sabbath to end at sundown so we could watch TV, or listen to the radio, or maybe drive to the projects to visit Aunt Bernice and our cousins. These were the cousins, I'd learn later, who had recently introduced Tim to marijuana, after which Tim introduced it to my twin and me. As soon as the Sabbath ended, we went to smoke some more.

STRANGE FRUIT

*L*eaving Erica wasn't easy. She was the first steady girlfriend I'd had in over a year, since I'd stopped using drugs. I understood that there was a correlation there; all of the eligible women I knew still got high, if only on a little pot now and then. But I'd quit it all, focusing instead on my new life as a person who could function in society without narcotics in his veins. I was taking college classes at Loop; I was making sober, law-abiding friends; I was paying my bills on time. But I could not get a girlfriend to save my life. The closest I'd come was Rita, one of the nurses at the medical center, with whom I had become good friends. But Rita was a married mother of four, so there were some limitations there. She was also white, and that posed a problem as well: I refused to date outside my race.

"That's stupid," Rita had said the first time I'd expressed this view. For the longest while she'd been trying to set me up with one of her white nurse colleagues. She wasn't trying to promote racial integration; there simply weren't many black nurses at the medical center, and the precious few there were probably wouldn't have dated a nonprofessional if he were the last brother on earth. Based on my observations, and on the rumor mill, the white nurses seemed to have shown some flexibility in this regard. "You mean to tell me," Rita continued, "that you won't date someone because of the color of her skin, just because she's white?"

"Yes."

"Why?"

"Because I'm not attracted to white women."

"Bullshit," she said.

"No, it's true," I insisted. But she knew I was lying. I'd told her many times I was attracted to her. The fact of the matter was I didn't want to be that stereotypical black man with the white girl-friend, the kind you see holding some bleached-blonde's hand and suspect harbors deep-rooted hatreds for his own race.

Like my friend Dale, for instance, who worked at the medical center too. Dale was into Chinese and Filipinas, and in a pinch he'd go for Puerto Ricans, but his obsession was white women, the finest and fairest, he'd told me, of them all. Every time I saw him he seemed to have a different one on his arm, and while his be-trayal saddened me, I admitted to a certain envy of his success. I made the mistake once of asking him his secret. "It's all about the penis," he'd said. He leaned back in his chair, looking very pleased, like he'd just revealed his new six-figure salary. "I just make sexual comments, you know, play up the wild-Zulu-warrior-of-the-jungle thing. From then on, it's like picking fruit off a tree. You should try it."

Had I wanted to take his advice, there was a great deal of fruit at my disposal. I was a "floater unit clerk," meaning I circulated among the wards from day to day, so I literally had hundreds of white nurses from whom to choose. It was to my advantage, too, that I was on friendly terms with many of them; sometimes we even ate our bag lunches together in the staff lounges. I knew, for instance, who was interested in sports, who was single, who was sleeping with which intern, and who, at any given moment, suf-fered from bloating and cramps. All of these topics had come up in various conversations, but the subject of my penis had never been broached, and I had no intention of broaching it.

And then I did an uncharacteristic thing, motivated, no doubt, by a bad seed Dale had planted in my subconscious. I was in a staff lounge—along with five white nurses, all of us in our early twenties—when the conversation turned to sex, as it sometimes had in the past. I don't recall exactly what precipitated my comment, only that it seemed the natural lead-in for me to interject, "Well, ladies, you know what they say about black men." The room filled with laughter, which lasted for several long seconds, as did the heat radiating off my cheeks.

"Pick the fruit," Dale urged me when I relayed this incident. "Pick the fruit right now." We were on the North Side, shopping for clothes that he said would aid me in my pursuit of female companionship. This was the ultra-cool part of Chicago, the epicenter of chic where open-air cafés ruled the strip and some of the restaurants had throw pillows instead of chairs. Almost everyone we passed was dressed head-to-toe in black—even though it was the height of summer—and soon I would be too. The bags I carried were filled with black pants, shirts, socks, and a pair of black shoes with soles so thick that they were disturbingly similar to the stacks I'd worn in the 1970s. I'd even bought a black leather biker's jacket, complete with half a dozen zippers and snaps, though Dale said I should wear it sparingly so as not to be typecast. Being typecast, he'd said before we went shopping, was my problem. "You always dress like a dork," he'd told me. I did not dispute this; dressing like a dork had been my goal. I was trying to blend in with all the other dorks around me, interns and medical students who never strayed from their oxford shirts and wrinkle-free khakis that fell far short of their penny loafers. My hope was to disguise the fact that I had been raised in the ghetto. Dale, who'd been raised in the ghetto too, insisted that the best disguise of all was a white girlfriend. An artsy outfit was a close second.

"I don't like it," Rita said when she saw my new look.

"Why not?"

"You look like a cat burglar in orthopedic shoes."

"No, seriously."

"Seriously."

"Yeah, well, all the other nurses like it."

She grinned. "Name *one* nurse who likes it."

Down the hall I saw Erica come out of a patient's room holding a jug of urine. "Erica," I said.

"*Erica?* That cute new blonde?"

I nodded. Rita looked unconvinced, so I added, "She told me I was hot in all-black."

Rita was laughing now, pausing to say, "She pities you." Her teasing was upsetting, but I played it cool, as my new look demanded. "She only said that," Rita continued, "because she's trying to make you feel better about being such a tool."

"If she thinks I'm such a tool," I said, "then . . . then . . . why did she ask me out for beer?" This was untrue, but it had the desired effect; all sound from Rita ceased. I closed the patient's chart I'd just taken a doctor's order from and walked away from the nurses' station.

A moment later, as I stood by the medicine cart transcribing the doctor's order, Erica came out of one of the patients' rooms and stood next to me. "What's up, Walker?" she asked.

"Not much," I said. "What's up with you?"

"Oh, God, don't ask," she responded, shaking her head. She was frazzled, as she always seemed to be. A very intense person, this Erica. "This day has been freaking crazy." She opened one of the medicine drawers, moved the contents around, then slammed it. She did this with three more drawers. "I hate it when the pharmacists don't deliver the meds to the right place." She huffed, blowing a long stream of air out of her mouth. I suspected she smoked, like me.

"Sounds like you could use a cigarette," I said.

"I'm dying for one."

"And a drink."

"Definitely."

I glanced toward the nurses' station. Rita was now leaning against the counter, looking my way with a mocking grin, having concluded, no doubt, that the bomb I'd dropped was filled not with napalm but with air. At first chance she'd confirm that with Erica. I decided to head her off at the pass. "So, Rita and I were talking, and, well, I told her that you and I were going out for a beer tonight. So if she asks, could you just tell her we are?"

I wasn't sure she heard me; she did not respond or look up from her pockets, which she was now riffling through. She found what she'd been searching for, a felt-tipped pen that she used to write on her left hand. Her left hand, I noticed, was covered in scribble. "Okay," she said. "A beer sounds great."

"Excuse me?"

She looked up. "A beer sounds great," she repeated. "I'd love to go."

So there, Rita, was my first thought. My second thought was, *Holy shit.*

It was a July night, and the air was thick with humidity and mosquitoes. I paced in front of the hospital smoking a cigarette, waiting for Erica to pick me up. I'd asked her if she wouldn't mind driving because my car was currently out of commission, which was to say rusting in some junkyard across town. No problem, she'd said. And then she suggested she pick me up at an exit used not by employees but for outpatients and visitors. No problem, I'd said.

I was more nervous than I could ever remember being. I tried to calm myself by thinking about how much Erica had laughed in the nurses' lounge when I'd made my sex joke, louder and longer, it seemed, than anyone else. But thinking about that only made me more nervous. Dale may have provided me with the secret to attract white women, but he had said nothing about what to do once they had arrived. There was also the matter of this being the first actual date of my life. I didn't even know where we should go.

The issue of where to go was put to rest, however, the moment I got in her Pinto. "I'm really not up for going to a bar," she said. And then she nonchalantly added, "Want to just hang out at your place?"

The fruit, it seemed, wasn't on a tree; it was lying on the ground at my feet. Which suggested some degree of overripeness. Overripeness was not what I was looking for. Not long-term anyway. But I supposed I could manage it for a night.

We first stopped at a liquor store for a six-pack of Heineken. Once at my apartment, we sat on my sofa talking, smoking, and drinking, the sexual tension between us vying for attention, it seemed to me, like a dog holding its leash. I kept looking for an opening in the conversation that would lead to a risqué comment, and perhaps from there to a kiss, but I could find no logical segue to my Zulu warrior from the topics at hand, her brother's meth addiction, for example, or her father's abandonment and alcoholism. The most I could contribute to the conversation were the dysfunctions of my family, topping those off, just to bring the conversation back to me, with a few of my own.

"I just can't believe that," she said. I'd just told her I used to be a dope fiend. "When did you stop?"

"About a year ago."

"Wow. I never would have guessed that. You just seem so together."

Well, I thought, *you know what they say about black men.* "I'm hardly together," I said. I chuckled. "I don't even own a car, really. I mean I do, technically, since the title's still in my dresser drawer, but . . ." My voice trailed off.

"Yeah, but you're taking college classes. And that's something." She leaned forward and patted my leg. "It's really impressive, the way you've turned your life around."

I winked. "Well, you know what they say?"

"What they say about what?"

"You know. Black men."

Her face dropped. She looked at her watch. "I need to get going. My roommate's probably wondering where I am." She rose and aggressively brushed off her white slacks, as if they were covered with cat hair, or biting ants. I offered to walk her to her car, a part of me waiting for her to say she was kidding, that she really wanted to remain with me, *right there in the jungle,* but by the time we'd gotten downstairs to where she'd parked, I accepted the fact she had actually come to talk. I resolved to attempt no more than a good-bye hug. And that, in an oddly satisfying way, was all we did. Afterward, I asked if she'd like to come back tomorrow. "Only," she said, "if you agree to spare me another black-man joke."

Dating a white woman was much different from what I expected, in that the dates consisted of staying in my apartment. For the first six weeks of our courtship, we never went anywhere, or did anything, that required us to be together outdoors. By the time I realized she didn't want to be seen in public with me, we'd been together for two months. I realized at the same time that I was completely okay with that, since I didn't want to be seen in public with her either.

And yet, despite how secretive we were—so secretive that we never acknowledged to each other that we were a couple—we somehow became fodder for the rumor mill at work. "Three people today alone asked me if Erica and I were seeing each other," I said to Dale. "I mean, how could anyone possibly know?"

"Easy," he said. "I told them."

"*What?*"

"Absolutely." He drank a sip of his Pepsi. We were having lunch in the cafeteria. "What's the point of dating a white woman if nobody knows?"

"The point," I said, "is to be with someone you like."

He snickered. "Oh, as if you like Erica."

"I do like her."

"And she likes you?"

"Yes."

"Then you shouldn't mind that I've told people you're a couple."

But I did mind, very much. Erica did too. She actually minded even more than me, which I found troubling. When I broke the news of our outing, she cursed and shook her head, and then sat on my couch and held her head between her hands, muttering to herself.

"So, um," I began, "is it really that awful for people to know you're dating me?"

"It's not that," she said.

"What is it?"

Silence.

"The fact that you're white and I'm black?" I asked.

More silence.

"I can't believe you would let race be an issue," I said.

"Oh, right," she responded as her head swung up. "Like it's not an issue with you."

"Well, it's not," I told her. "Not one bit. The question here is, why is it an issue for you." Her chin began to quiver; I had struck a sensitive chord. So I pressed on. "Maybe it's time for you to take a good hard look at yourself, Erica. Maybe it's time for you to confront whatever demons you have about race. Because if you're not ready to do that, then I think it's time for us to end this, right here, right now." I folded my arms over my chest, hoping she'd say, *Yes, let's end this, right here, right now,* because, after my conversation with Dale, I had already confronted my demons, and my demons had won.

I had not lied when I said I liked Erica very much. I already knew she was one of the best things that had happened to me in a long time. But I just could not handle the thought of walking down the street with her, arm in arm, fielding the disapproving stares of passersby. I couldn't deal with the thought of black men like Dale grinning my way before casting a sly, congratulatory wink, or black women shaking their heads in disgust and mouthing the word *traitor*. And then there were my relatives, especially my aunt Bernice, whose opinion of white people was less than favorable. No, better to break it off right now, I decided. Better to end it before we were in too deep.

But the fact that we were both crying suggested we already were.

We had our first heart-to-heart that night, confessing our apprehensions about being an interracial couple. Chicago had a well-earned reputation as the most segregated big city in the country, which meant there would be many places we could not comfortably go, and some places we couldn't go at all. It was complicated enough for her to visit me in my all-black neighborhood, though it was true that my lease would be ending soon and I could move. There was also the matter that certain members of her family would not be thrilled at our union, and neither would some of my family, like Aunt Bernice, or some of our colleagues and friends. But it was equally true that a number of people from each of these groups would be happy for us and supportive.

Then the conversation turned to race in more general terms. We talked about how racism had harmed so much in this country, how it had wrecked and even ended countless lives. And we spoke of how it wasn't long ago that a black man's real or imagined interest in a white woman was an occasion for a lynching, and that led us to conclude that we, in a very personal way, were faced with the opportunity to make a grand stand against bigotry.

It was all quite idealistic, in retrospect, the way we convinced ourselves that our union was a form of social activism, the civil rights movement on a miniature scale. Even four years later, when we walked down the street hand in hand, or sat hugging in the bleachers of Wrigley Field, or when we went to museums, or to the theater, or attended open-air concerts along the shore, I sometimes still imagined that the people frowning at us were ready to toss a brick our way in the name of intolerance and hate. And then I would ease Erica a little closer and fix my gaze on something in the distance, something high above their heads.

And I wonder, sometimes, if I would be still doing that now, had Erica and I not said our tearful good-byes as I left for Iowa City.

DISOBEDIENCE

*F*or nearly six months after she was born, my mother's left eye was sealed tight with thick, yellow mucus. It was probably a severe case of conjunctivitis, treated in 1936 with a warm compress and boric acid, unless you were uneducated, rural, black, and southern, like my grandparents. They tried pee. Four drops, to be exact, from the first urine of the day. When that did not work, they tried blowing a stream of cigar smoke on the pupil, and when that failed they covered it with ash from the hearth, and then a few drops of gasoline, and then saliva, and then flour—all of this over the course of six months until at last the tide of mucus receded and left a small, gray stone.

That was the first half of my mother's eyesight-losing story; she reminded me of the second half after asking me if Tim and Jimmy were smoking pot.

"They would never smoke pot," I lied.

"Are you sure, Jerry?"

"No. I mean, yes."

She was quiet for a moment. "If you find out they're smoking it, I want you to tell me."

I didn't respond.

"Will you tell me, Jerry?"

"Okay."

"Always obey your mother," she said.

"Yes, ma'am."

"Never forget that. Always obey your mother." And then, as proof of why this obedience must be so, she took me back to Arkansas, the spring of 1945. She is nine and standing in the parlor with her hands on her hips, scowling across the room at her mother, who is on her knees scrubbing the pinewood floor. My mother wants to go outside, but there are chores for her to perform, such as picking up after her eight older siblings and caring for her eight younger ones. My mother makes her plea once again. When it too is denied she runs out the door, jumps off the porch, and heads toward an open field where children are playing among the grazing cattle. She looks over her shoulder and doesn't dwell on her mother's face because she doesn't know it is the last time she will see it. Instead, the look is quick and general, just long enough to confirm that her mother has chased her no farther than the porch, and for the horse-drawn wagon passing in front of the house to stop.

June Bug is driving, the two-by-four plank he's sitting on jutting far off the right side. He feels it jolt beneath him, but when he looks to his right it's too late to see his little sister's head snap back and her wide bare feet swoop toward the sky.

My mother's hands fill with blood and what's left of her vision. She tries to put it all back inside, but there is no use, so she screams instead, just as her screaming mother reaches her.

"Always obey your mother," my mother said once more.

"I will."

She rose from where she'd sat next to me on the bed and walked toward the door, pausing just short of it to face me. "Have you cleaned your room like I asked you?"

"No, ma'am."

"I suggest you do so."

"Yes, ma'am," I said.

When I finished cleaning my room, I went downstairs for a

glass of lemonade. Tommy and Linda were at the kitchen table playing Scrabble. I watched the game for a second before I took a glass from the cupboard, nearly dropping it at the sound of a tremendous crash. All three of us rushed to the hall, where our father had fallen and now lay convulsing. Our mother arrived a second later, guided by the sound of his choking. Tommy ran to call an ambulance while Linda ran back into the kitchen for a spoon. She was already crying as she returned to hand it to our mother, who used it to pry open my father's clenched teeth before forcing in a pill. All the while I'd stood hovering over them both, wanting to help but knowing there was nothing I could do. At last my mother rose up from my father, her job completed. This was the part of his seizures when we waited to see if he would live or die.

The back door suddenly swung open. Tim and Jimmy bounded up the stairs, halting their uproarious laugher at the sight of the mayhem. Their eyes were watery and bloodshot, as if they, like Linda, like me, had been crying.

ORIENTATION

*T*he rock music was troubling but not as much as the beer. It was warm, flat, musty, and seemed to have left a white residue in the bottom of my cup. My roommate Lenny tried to allay my concerns. "It's just spoiled milk!" he yelled over an electric guitar, which screeched from the eight speakers in the ten-by-ten room. Lenny aimed his thumb to our left at the five students huddled before a video game. "These guys aren't known for washing their dishes!" He hoisted his plastic cup in the air and added, "That's why I brought my own! Next time you'll be wanting to do the same!" A cheer went up and we looked at the television, where a combatant fired a heroic final shot from his bazooka before his body toppled over, next to his head. It seemed a good time to leave. I sat my cup on the floor near the keg and quietly slipped into the hall, wondering, as I headed for my room, what I'd gotten myself into.

Two years earlier, when I began making preparations to transfer to The University of Iowa, I was convinced it was the best decision I'd ever made. And it was, right up until the moment I arrived, when it was trumped by the worst decision I'd ever made—not finding off-campus housing. Even if my dorm had not been crawling with white males almost ten years my junior, I was not a people person. I disliked crowds, parties, male bonding, large social gatherings of any kind, which seemed to be the sole purpose of dormitory life. Toss in some incessant Led Zeppelin and barrels of Milwaukee Lite, and this was not an ideal situation.

Because Lenny had flinched at the sight of me entering our room, I knew I wouldn't have to worry about him wanting us to hang out together. But he had felt compelled to introduce me to some of his friends, who had also flinched when I entered their room before handing me a cup of beer and resuming their obliteration of mankind. I'd been in town just a few hours and already I was miserable. It would have helped if I could have reached the outside world, but I hadn't been provided with the access code necessary to make long-distance calls from my room. I wasn't sure where to get one of these codes, and Lenny could not remember where he'd gotten his. I went to bed that night in a state of high anxiety and doubt, ripe conditions for a nightmare.

I dreamed I was trapped in the medical center where I'd once worked, running from ward to ward, searching for and unable to find an exit. The building wasn't on fire, as it often was in this recurrent dream, but gang-bangers were again chasing me with weapons. Normally the weapons were knives and guns; this time they were bazookas. My head was blown off at exactly 5:17 AM, the moment my eyes opened to see the glowing digits of the alarm clock on my desk. The sky had not yet begun to brighten, but the low-wattage light seeping in from the hall allowed me to see the person standing in the center of the room, peeing on the recliner.

Two hours later I was sitting at my desk, working on a short story, when Lenny woke and inquired about the smell.

"Some guy peed on the recliner," I said.

He rolled onto his back and wiggled his forefingers against his closed eyes. "You must have left the door unlocked."

I noted that he'd come in after me, but then I remembered that at some point during the night I had gone to the men's room across the hall. I apologized.

"That's okay," he responded. "But from now on, you'll be wanting to remember to lock it."

I turned my attention back to my short story, finally hitting a groove just before Lenny switched on his television. I shut down my word processor and gathered some toiletries for a shower. As I was about to leave the room, Lenny looked away from some game show and pointed toward my bare feet. "You'll be wanting to get some flip-flops, like, immediately."

"Why?"

"Trust me," he said.

In addition to the private shower stalls, there was a communal bathing area, which could hold at least twenty people, the approximate number in there now. From what I could tell as I brushed my teeth nearby at the sink, these twenty naked people were having a normal conversation about normal things—classes they would be taking, the Hawkeyes' chances in the Rose Bowl, what they'd done over winter break—as if they weren't naked at all, or as if the university were actually a giant nudist colony. Or maybe this was just the kind of thing white males did. As I headed toward one of the private stalls, I remembered hearing something about how white boys coming of age would masturbate together, standing in a circle and betting on who would complete the deed first, and then I cursed myself once more for not finding off-campus housing. I would do so late in the spring. But I would get some flip-flops immediately.

I left my dorm a little after nine to attend one of two orientations, the first of which was for midyear transfer students. In my backpack was a map of the vast campus that, an hour later, as I struggled to find my way, I had not yet removed for fear of appearing lost. For the same reason, I also did not ask directions of any of the people I passed, and there were hundreds of them, it seemed, maybe thousands, as one might expect in downtown Chicago, except that in downtown Chicago you'd see some black faces now and then. If I hadn't received the letter requiring me to attend a mandatory orientation for minorities, I might have concluded I was the only one. Or if I hadn't first stopped in my dorm's cafeteria.

There, in the center of the room, stranded among the sea of white faces, a dozen black students had sat crammed at a table designed for four. I'd wondered if they were all longtime friends, perhaps arriving from a single remote high school in the Deep South where Jim Crow was still the law of the land. What would happen, I wondered, if a white student tried to sit with them, or if a black student refused? I discovered the latter after I'd paid for my breakfast and found an empty table in the far corner. I was halfway finished with my omelet when four of the black students—two males, two females—came to recruit me.

"How you doing today, my brother?" one of the males asked.

"Been better," I said. "Been worse."

"We noticed you're sitting here by yourself."

"That's true."

"You waiting on anyone in particular?"

I shook my head and filled my mouth with egg and cheese.

"Well, you should come on over and join us then."

I glanced at their table; three more black students had arrived. "What for?" I asked.

"What for? *What for?* Why do you *think*, brother?"

I hunched my shoulders. "To help break some sort of Guinness record?"

They exchanged smirks. One of the women put her hands on her hips as she spoke: "Obviously, you have something against your own people." With that, the envoys went back to their table, where words were exchanged, followed by headshakes and rolled eyes. I finished my breakfast and left.

The building for transfer orientation eluded me for thirty more minutes, but at last I cornered it near the banks of the river that wound through campus. I went to the section where

English majors were being advised, the most crowded section of all. It took me a while to find an adviser who was free, a thirty-something-year-old woman with dark circles under her eyes and a profound look of sadness. I got the sense that she had decided to stop smiling many years ago, though the urge seemed to have returned when I showed her my tentative schedule.

"Now, what possessed you," she asked, emitting a faint chuckle, "to choose all English courses?"

Because I'm an English major, I thought, but, believing this to be a trick question, I didn't reply. Instead, I tried to outsmile her, which was easy enough to do; after a few seconds of our clownish duel her lips flatlined again.

"Classes start tomorrow," she continued, "which of course means that *all* of the English courses are full. You'll have to choose something else." She pushed my registration form across the table toward me.

I pushed it back. "You don't understand," I said. "I moved here from Chicago specifically in order to take English classes."

"Sorry," she said, pushing the paper toward me once more.

I pushed it back again before playing my ace card: "I came here to be a writer."

Her smile returned for a brief second and then vanished. She slid my form to me a final time. "The bottom line is that our English courses always fill within hours of *early* registration. This is *late* registration." My only option, she said, was to take some of my General Education requirements, like math, physical education, or a science, courses I could have taken at Loop Community College for less than a hundred dollars each. Here they were going to cost me thousands.

I stormed from the building feeling like I'd arrived in some unpleasant foreign country; that the idyllic, friendly campus I'd visited four months ago was a prop, staged and orchestrated to make me feel welcome, right down to the warmth and sun. At the moment it was cold and snowing. The first few flakes had begun soon after I left the cafeteria. Now they descended with such abundance that I didn't see that the traffic light I passed wasn't green. An SUV nearly hit me when I stepped off the curb, causing me to slip and fall as I hastily retreated. Three passersby came to my aid, helping me stand.

"That was a pretty nasty spill," one of them said.

"Are you hurt?" asked another.

"No, I'm okay," I responded, holding my throbbing wrist. "I'm fine."

"Are you sure?"

"Yes." I smiled at them as I had at the adviser, and they smiled back before leaving.

I took a quick peek at my map. It seemed that if I stayed on the street I was on, I wouldn't miss the building I sought. And yet somehow I did. I found myself in a residential community with tattered couches on the porches and empty Bud Lite cans being buried in the snow. I retraced my steps, rechecked the map, saw that I'd read it upside down, and started out again. A short while later I gave up and asked someone for help. He pointed to the building next to where we stood.

Once inside I headed to the basement, where the room for the minority orientation was located. The forty or so students already there represented a variety of races, though they were uniformly young, probably no older than eighteen. They sat rigidly in their chairs, facing the unattended podium and poised to take notes. I flopped down in one of the seats in the rear, my frustrations piled high like a pyramid of kindling, waiting for a spark. As soon as an African American male in a three-piece suit approached the podium, I raised my hand. "Excuse me," I said.

The man looked up; everyone else turned to face me. "A question already," he said with a wide grin. "Please be patient, young man, until after my presentation."

I lowered my hand and managed to keep it down through his introduction of his staff. Then I raised it again.

"Young man," he said. "I *promise* we'll get to you as soon as the presentation is over."

This time I was able to keep my hand down for a full ten minutes, even during his comments about how difficult life could be for minorities on a predominantly white campus. When he began talking about how isolated and inferior we might feel, I distracted myself by counting the ceiling panels. Humming song lyrics proved to be a pretty effective sound barrier, but somehow it was penetrated by the words *disenfranchised* and *social outcasts*.

I rose and cleared my throat.

The speaker stopped. Everyone looked at me again.

"Young man, what *is* the problem?"

I explained that I had not been able to get into any English classes, that I did not have a long-distance access code, and that I was in dire need of flip-flops. Judging from the fact that a member of the staff was suddenly ushering me from the room, I had aired my concerns with a considerable degree of hysteria. In the hall, the staff member spoke to me very soothingly for several minutes, promising to get me an access code and to do what she could to find me at least one English course. "And don't you worry about those flip-flops," she said, rubbing her hand up and down my arm. "We'll get those for you too. Right now you just continue taking deep breaths, honey. You just breathe, nice and easy, and everything will be fine."

Late that evening, with my new access code in hand, I called Professor Homewood, described how the day had gone, and told him I was leaving.

"By all means, you should," he said. "I'd come get you myself, dear boy, if I had a car, or a space-traveling machine." I heard a faint clink, ice cubes colliding, I knew, along a wave of scotch. I'd caught him at a bad time. I decided I would call him back in the morning, perhaps from the lobby of the Greyhound station. I hung up and was about to start packing when my roommate noted that it was 10:00 PM.

"And?"

"Tomorrow's a school day," he said.

"And?"

"Lights-out time."

All signs pointed to a night in the medical center with bazooka-toting gang-bangers, and as soon as I fell asleep, there they were. I lapped the oncology ward twice with Vice Lords and Black Gangster Disciples on my heels before locking myself in a utility closet. Crouched in the corner, I waited for them to burst through the door, but all they did was knock politely, a faint rhythmic drumming that continued even after I'd forced myself awake. "Who could that be?" I heard my roommate grumble, and then I realized that the door being knocked on was ours. I looked at my clock; it was nearly midnight. After a brief pause, the knocking continued. I rose to see who it was, expecting to come face-to-face with the pisser, but instead there were two white males, one with a six-inch-long beard, the other with the hair and glasses of John Lennon.

Their names were Aaron and Charles. Like me, they had come to Iowa City because of the Writers' Workshop. They had seen me at transfer orientation, overheard my conversation with the adviser, which had gone pretty much like theirs, and then spent the rest of the day going room-to-room, tracking me down to have a beer. That struck me as a bizarre thing to do, more than a little neurotic. So I accepted their offer.

We bought a six-pack and drank it in the laundry room, located in the basement of my dorm, which would become our frequent gathering place. When we weren't there discussing the stories we were working on, we were attending readings of the famous and want-to-be-famous, imagining ourselves at the microphone sharing with the audience the prose that we shared with one another.

Our alliance continued until halfway through the semester, and then it abruptly ended when Charles's girlfriend in Montana called to say she was pregnant with his child. He left on the next flight. But by then I felt at home. Aaron and I had met a few other budding writers. We attended all the local readings. We loitered in used-book stores. And in the late spring we found rooms to rent in a rustic commune for artists and hippies, a place where, instead of electric guitars, tambourines and love poems filled the night air.

I do not know where Aaron and Charles are now. I do not know what became of their lives. I have not seen either of them in fifteen long years, not even in one of my nightmares, where I would not be surprised if they arrived, in some terrible final scene, to save me.

REAL

*T*im wanted us to try our hand at selling. We were in our garage, as usual, only this time a mountain of marijuana was before us on a newspaper. Some of it had been stuffed into little envelopes that would go for five or ten dollars. There were dozens of one-dollar joints, too; we were helping him roll those as he spoke about the big money there was to be made. He was making a lot of it at the Illinois Institute of Technology, and there was a lot of it to be made at South Shore High, which, after just a few days of being freshmen, Jimmy and I had discovered was full not only of thugs but also of potheads. But Jimmy wasn't interested in being a dealer. I wasn't either. So Tim changed the subject. "You boys have any pussy yet?" he asked.

Lately he was always asking us about pussy. It made me uncomfortable, because I had not had any yet, and Tim seemed to think it was important that we have some very soon, as if it were on the verge of all being gone. I don't remember what I said— probably no, because lying was strictly prohibited by our church, too, and I wasn't yet comfortable with multitasking sins. While we got high, Tim told us about all the different races of women he'd slept with at his college, an impressive variety due to the international appeal of the sciences. "And the Asian girls have pussies that slant sideways," he said. "Squinty, like their eyes." I made a mental note that, when I did at last lose my virginity, it should not be with an Asian girl. It never occurred to me that Tim was lying. I never doubted anything he said.

When all the weed had been packaged and rolled, Tim told us he had to make a delivery. Jimmy and I decided to go inside the house and trip out playing pool. We entered the back door, burst into giggles when it creaked, and went straight into the basement. We'd been playing for a few minutes when, from behind me, Jesus called us sinners. I whirled around and was relieved to see that I was mistaken; it was only Tommy, clutching his Bible and looking crazed. He accused us of being high. Jimmy told him to shut up. Tommy's eyes widened before he lunged forward. Instantly they were fighting, fists and pool sticks swinging everywhere, creating such a commotion that it brought our father into the basement, moving toward the fracas with outstretched arms. Linda appeared at the top of the stairs with a hand over her mouth, and a second later our mother joined her, asking what was happening, what in God's name was going on. Our father was yelling now and so were Jimmy and Tommy, who had finally separated. "I want to know who started this!" our father was saying. "He attacked me!" Jimmy was saying, and Tommy was saying, "They're on drugs! Tim is getting them high! They're on drugs!" Jimmy and I denied it, swore it wasn't true. Our father believed us, or sided with us; I still don't know which and I still don't know why. All I know is that he ordered Tommy to pack his things and leave.

When Tim came home late that night, Jimmy told him what had happened.

"That's what he gets," I added, "for being a sissy."

"Don't say that," Tim rebuked me. "Tommy's your brother."

"But . . . but," I stammered.

Tim cut me off with a wave of his hand. "Tommy was just

trying to look out for you," he said, "but there's some crazy stuff going on out there in those streets that he just doesn't understand. But *I* do." He put his arm around my shoulders. "I'll look out for you now, little bro'. I'll show you what's real."

And I believed that too.

CHAMELEONS

*I*t was June 1991, and I was sitting outside in the quad at the University of Illinois at Chicago, reading a book on sadomasochistic porn. Five similar books were spread around me in the grass, their raunchy covers absorbing the midday sun. I'd glanced up from the one in my hands and she was standing over me, a girl I guessed to be sixteen. One of those AP high school students, I figured, taking a college class, something in sociology that required her to conduct random interviews around campus. I decided that I would have a little fun with her, claim that I was a graduate student completing my PhD, since, at age twenty-seven, I was old enough for this to be true.

"You're in the program, aren't you?" she asked.

"Yes indeed," I said. "I am in the program."

"I thought so."

I smiled.

She smiled back and said, "I am too."

My jaw dropped. "You're . . . you're getting your PhD?"

"That's the plan."

She was smarter than I thought. "How old are you?" I asked. "Fifteen? Sixteen?"

"Twenty-one, actually."

I said I didn't believe her. She laughed and set down her book bag and then reached inside it to remove a wallet. She showed me her driver's license, pointing a glossy fingernail to her birth date. She *was* twenty-one, though I was less curious about her age now than the photo of the white woman next to her ID. She saw me looking at it. "Oh, that's my mother," she explained, and then, as if she'd been asked questions about her ethnicity a million times, she added in the same breath, "my father's black. Or African. Zimbabwean, to be specific." She paused and extended her hand. "Pardon my manners," she said. "I'm Brenda Molife. And you're Jerry Walker, right?"

"How . . . how did you know that?"

"I heard it when you were introduced yesterday at orientation."

And then everything clicked. She, like me, was in the Summer Research Opportunity Program: a three-month-long internship designed to prepare minority undergraduates for the rigors of graduate school. Which meant that she was no more a doctoral student than I was. Which also meant that the two of us—along with a dozen other students—would be spending a lot of time together in the coming months. I looked at her again, really for the first time, and saw that she was quite pretty, beautiful, in fact. I asked her if she'd like to get lunch.

"That would be nice," she said. "But I can't. I have an appointment. I'm headed to my apartment now to get ready for it."

"You don't live on campus?"

"No, not anymore." She mentioned a street that I knew wasn't far away. I asked if I could walk her there, claiming the need to stretch my legs. When she consented, I rose and started gathering my books. She picked one up for me, pausing to look at the cover—a woman in thigh-high leather boots, a leather bodice, leather gloves that rose to her armpits; she held a whip and wore a mask. The title, which I noticed Brenda mouthed, was, *The*

Sadeian Woman: And the Ideology of Pornography. Now she looked at me and squinted, as if DANGEROUS PSYCHOPATH were written in tiny print across my forehead.

"I can explain that," I said.

As we walked toward her apartment, I made a case for my normalcy, noting that the books were the property of the professor with whom I'd been paired. This professor was interested in the portrayal of women in pornographic literature. I was not. But I was very much interested in the three-thousand-dollar stipend I would be earning working with her, as well as the free dorm housing for the summer. The only drawback was that the housing was here in Chicago, a city to which I'd vowed never to return when I left five months earlier to attend the University of Iowa. I could have stayed in Iowa City as I'd wanted, since the University of Iowa sponsored this program too, but I wasn't aware of that when a friend at UIC mailed me an application. And so there I was, back in Chicago for the summer due to a silly oversight, talking to the woman I would someday marry.

"Do you like Iowa City?" Brenda asked.

"Not at first," I confessed. "But it's grown on me. There's a really cool, laid-back lifestyle, sort of like a giant Woodstock."

"Seems like you're right at home," she said, her gaze sweeping over my attire. I was wearing tattered Birkenstock sandals, faded cargo shorts, tie-dyed T-shirt, and sunglasses with round, near impenetrable black lenses. A bandanna was wrapped around my brow. "It's a good look," she added, nodding. "Refreshingly uncommon."

She, I learned as we talked, was refreshingly uncommon, too. I hadn't met any black women who studied art history and had traveled overseas; they had not loved theater, mystery novels, museums, Bach, U2, and INXS; nor had they been raised in white suburbia and played the violin and oboe; and they certainly had not exclaimed "Gosh!" when caught off guard by a belch, as Brenda had just done, lifting her small hand to her lips and turning deep red. "Pardon me," she murmured, glancing bashfully in my direction just as a wad of bubblegum attached itself to my sandal. As I swore and dragged my foot along the sidewalk, Disney's *Lady and the Tramp* came to mind.

The front door to her apartment was wedged between a bakery and a pizzeria. She stood before it now, rummaging in her backpack for her keys. A siren blared and we both looked to where a police car zoomed by with twirling lights. We were on Taylor Street, a busy thoroughfare in the heart of Little Italy. The medical center, where I'd wasted nearly ten years of my life, stood in the distance, sending me bad vibes every time I glanced its way. "Well," Brenda said, keys in hand, "thank you for walking me home."

"My pleasure," I responded, and then, inexplicably, I gave her a little wave, with just my fingers, like I was casting some kind of spell on her. If I *could* have cast a spell on her, it would have been to make her believe that I was respectful and free of perversions and entirely worthy of seeing her again. But I was certain I'd given just the opposite impression. Already feeling dejected, I turned and began walking away, spinning back around when she called my name.

"You never told me how old *you* are," she said.

"I'm . . . um . . . I'm twenty-seven."

She squinted at my forehead again, this time to read, MUCH, MUCH TOO OLD TO BE AN UNDERGRADUATE.

"I can explain that," I said.

But it seemed I wouldn't get the chance. In the week that followed, she attended none of our program's mandatory meetings, she was never in the office she'd been assigned, and I never saw her around campus. And so, on the eighth day, I retraced my steps to her apartment. For the longest time I studied the buzzers on the mailboxes, none of which had a corresponding name, and I wondered if they had been like that before or if she'd had the names removed in case I returned. I took a piece of paper and a pen from my backpack and wrote, "Hi, Brenda. I'd like to see you again. Please call me." After adding my name and number, I used the gum I was chewing to affix the note to the door. Even before I made it back to my dorm, I was convinced she would think I was a stalker, because gumming notes to apartment building doors was the kind of thing a stalker would do.

Another week passed and still nothing. When I wasn't reading in the quad where we'd met, hoping she'd walk by, I was in my sweltering dorm room, hoping she'd call.

At last she did, ten days after I'd left the note.

Her roommate had found it, she told me, purely by chance because the tenants usually entered the apartment through the back stairs in the alley. When I asked why she hadn't been around, she revealed her secret: She had a second internship at the Art Institute, where she was calling me from now. Our program forbade second internships. Lady, it seemed, was a bit of a rule breaker, which the Tramp found more than a little attractive.

"So," I said, "I'll be headed either there to have lunch with you, or to the undergraduate research director's office to have you fired." When she did not respond, I laughed to let her know I was kidding. She still didn't respond. "I'm kidding," I said.

"That's an interesting sense of humor you have," she noted.

I admitted it took some getting used to.

Forty-five minutes later we were eating onion rings and french fries while I explained the making of a twenty-seven-year-old college junior, including my various incarnations along the way, the most recent as a hippie. Had she met me a year earlier, I told her, I would have been dressed in all-black like a connoisseur or producer of high art. Before that I was a prep; I'd amassed an impressive wardrobe of pastel-colored polos and blue cotton Dockers, topping everything off with argyle socks and penny loafers that I'd accessorized with actual pennies. On chilly days I'd draped a wool sweater over my back, its thick sleeves crossed over my neck, choking me like some headless mugger as I pranced through the ghetto. Before that I'd worn narrow ties and two-piece suits, impersonating the businessmen I'd seen on the cover of *Black Enterprise,* and before that, in my teens, I'd worn the hand-me-downs of my brother Tim, whose fashion idols were pimps, though his income was derived mainly from selling drugs. Most of the silk shirts and polyester slacks he'd given me were filled with reefer burns, and even though they were difficult to detect, on account of the multitude and boldness of colors, they were a nice change from the jeans and T-shirts I'd worn, the couture of choice for delinquents, which I hesitantly admitted to Brenda I'd once been.

"Wait a minute," she said, reaching for one of my fries. "I don't get how being a prep fits into all of this."

"That was when I worked at the medical center. All the doctors dressed that way, so I did too."

"You're quite the chameleon."

"I know. I have this bad habit of trying to blend in."

She took another french fry and said, "Do not get me started about trying to blend in."

But I had gotten her started, and over the next thirty minutes I learned that she was quite the chameleon too. First she was African, born in Zambia, living on a diet rich in maize and speaking her father's Bantu tongue. And then she was a four-year-old American living in a Chicago suburb, just another of the community's little white girls, only with a slightly richer tan. But then puberty arrived, bringing with it a fleet of boys who, unfortunately for her, were interested in girls with tans of a more transient kind. By the time she was eighteen, she'd had only one boyfriend. If that was going to change, she knew, she'd have to attend a college where there was a large percentage of blacks, and then, once there, she'd have to become black too.

She chose UIC, whose student body was 9 percent African American; by the end of her first year, she knew many of them. She'd joined the black student union, started listening to gangsta rap, declared a minor in black studies, attended three stomping contests, participated in four black clubs, and modeled in the black fashion show. She selected fried chicken in the cafeteria instead of the Jell-O mold and never left her dorm room without her FREE MANDELA button. And she did get boyfriends. But after a while her suitors concluded she was an imposter, no more African American than a white actress in a minstrel show. One after the other, they left her for the real thing—coeds who were either *all* black or *all* white, a single race in both appearance and manner, in both substance and style.

Being interracial had made her life difficult, filled it with so much confusion, alienation, and self-doubt that I could barely contain my excitement as she talked. Here was a woman, I was convinced, who would understand me. My hand trembled as I pushed the napkins closer to her. She took one and dabbed the corners of her eyes. "I'm sorry," she said. "It's just all so upsetting. People can be so superficial sometimes, so *cruel.*"

"And *opportunistic,*" I added. I ate one of her onion rings. "So," I asked, "what are you doing tomorrow?"

We spent the next day together. And the one after that. And then every day right through August, going from being strangers to friends to a couple in love. But it would all be over in two weeks, when the research program came to an end, because I'd return to Iowa City while she'd remain to start her senior year. We both agreed that a long-distance relationship simply wouldn't work, a clearheaded, rational conclusion reached two months earlier before we fully understood our bond. We still didn't fully understand it, but I had a theory.

I presented it to her one day as we walked arm in arm along Michigan Avenue's magnificent mile, window-shopping. We'd been dating for ten weeks by then, about the time it had taken me to deconstruct our relationship in a way that went far beyond our mutual attraction, deeper than our enjoyment of documentaries and long novels, beyond our obsession with Indian food, watching

This Old House, and staring through panes of glass at things we couldn't afford.

"So let me make sure I have this right," she said. "My being black is the same thing as you being a thug?"

"Exactly." We paused to look at a dining room set. She pointed at the silverware and then looked at me, seeking my opinion. I shook my head; too art deco. We continued walking. I went on with my theory. "But deep down inside, we both knew we were imposters. Frauds. That we were both just searching to discover who we really were."

"So, who are we now?"

"I'm a stalker."

She smiled. "And me?"

"You're Dorian Gray. The female version, forever sixteen."

She stopped walking. We were in front of Neiman Marcus, which was too expensive for us to even window-shop. "What an amazing dress," she whispered, staring up at the mannequin, which wore a beige satin gown that fell just below the knees, with lace circling the bustline and hem.

"You ought to try it on."

"Should I?"

"Why not? Besides, it's sweltering out here. Some air-conditioning would feel pretty good right now."

"That's true," she said. I followed her inside.

We wandered around for a moment, looking through the racks of gowns for the one in the window, until a spirited saleslady approached us. "Hello, hello, *hel-lo!*" she sang. "What can I help you with, darlings?"

"May I please see that gown?" Brenda asked, pointing toward the window.

The saleslady gasped. "That would look so *astonishing* on you!" She took Brenda's hand and pulled her away. I headed for an empty chair near the dressing room, where a group of men with miserable expressions had gathered. Before them twenty-five or so women drifted from rack to rack, bees in a field of lilies. One of the men grumbled something about the Cubs, igniting a bitter discussion in which we all joined. I was going on about the awful pitching when Brenda called my name. I looked at her and lost my breath. The saleslady was next to her, glowing like a proud mother. "Doesn't she look *amazing*!" she exclaimed. Before I could agree, the saleslady charged off toward another customer, shouting back over her shoulder: "That would make such a gorgeous *wedding dress*!"

All the women in the area froze. They looked at Brenda, cupped their hands to their cheeks, and suddenly they were upon her.

"Congratulations!" they squealed, and then they told her she would make a lovely bride, asked about the big day, hugged her, wiped their eyes, spun her around, dug pictures of their own weddings out of their purses. At one point Brenda looked toward me for help, but there was nothing I could do, other than hunch my shoulders, just as one of them was forcibly clutched. I turned to face my assailant.

"You must be the lucky groom-to-be!" he bellowed. "Good luck to you, buddy!" The other men began slapping my back and shaking my hand, and someone reached inside his blazer and pulled out a long thick cigar. Now I looked to Brenda for help, but she was deep inside the circle of buzzing women, out of view. As the men started offering me tawdry advice, the saleslady came hurrying back toward the mob of women, wondering what was going on.

"This young lady is getting married!" one of the women told her.

The saleslady rested a hand just above her bosom. "Well bless her *soul*! And to think I helped find the perfect dress! I'll just ring that up for you, then, as soon as you're ready."

Her mouth agape, Brenda looked at me, silently imploring me to say something.

I said, "Gosh."

A moment later, a chorus of well wishes accompanied us out the door. The wedding dress was in a garment bag, draped over Brenda's arm. The cigar was between my lips. We stumbled along the magnificent mile dazed and speechless for several minutes before Brenda asked me what had just happened. I told her I wasn't sure. All I knew was that we'd walked into the store as boyfriend and girlfriend, our romance intense but nearing its end, and we'd walked out engaged and bound for life, changed, just like that, into the next thing we'd be. I reached for her hand.

SISSIES

*T*here were about twelve of us, the honor students of the freshman class, and we'd been quarantined for our own protection. We could not take courses with the non-honor-students. We were advised not to socialize with them. I'd figured out on my own that eye contact should be avoided, especially as we marched together from one class to the next, which we were about to do now. After gathering our books, we approached the door with slow, halting steps, as if waiting on the other side was the hangman's noose.

The hall was crowded with students punching and shoving one another, laughing, slamming lockers, applying lipstick, shooting imaginary balls in the air, flashing gang signs—activities I stole peeks at as we hurried by. We'd nearly reached our destination when someone spotted us and yelled to make way for the nerds, sparking a smattering of "punks," "chumps," and "sissies." I was pretty certain it was Jimmy who'd called us sissies, but I didn't look up to confirm it.

This was one of the very reasons why I'd decided not to attend the magnet college preparatory school that my teachers had urged me to attend since I was twelve. No one else I knew had the grades to be accepted there, and I didn't like the idea of being singled out, especially as a geek. And yet thanks to the honors program at

South Shore, it had happened anyway, so now I had to do something to try to fit in; such was my thinking when I arrived on campus one fall morning with my backpack full of marijuana.

I spotted a group of boys in the parking lot, talking near the hood of a Camaro. They fell quiet as they watched me approach.

"Got that fire weed," I said; this was the phrase Tim had taught me.

"Oh yeah?" said one of the boys.

I nodded.

"Got a dime bag?"

I reached into my backpack, took out a dime bag, and handed it to him.

"How about some papers?" he asked.

I nodded again and dug some from my rear pocket. I gave them to the boy. He tore two sheets free and gave back the rest. Then we stood there quietly as he proceeded to roll a joint until I finally got the nerve to ask him for payment. "That'll be ten dollars, please," I said.

The other boys chuckled. My customer continued sprinkling some of the weed onto the papers.

"Ten dollars," I repeated.

The joint was rolled now. I watched as it was slipped between the boy's chapped lips. Now the boy patted his pockets, searching, I assumed, for a light. I had one but I didn't offer it. One of his friends handed him some matches. He lit the joint, took a deep drag, and then held his breath for a few seconds before blasting the smoke from his nostrils like a cartoon bull. "Hey," he began, "this *is* that fire weed." They all burst into laughter. I turned and left.

A short while later I entered a bathroom where six upperclassmen were shooting dice. "Got that fire weed," I said. The boys looked up. "Got that fire weed," I said again. A chubby kid leapt to his feet and was upon me before I could react. He threw me to the floor and began punching me, and then they all joined in. Hands rummaged through my pockets and my backpack while others continued swinging. After a final blow to my chin, the boys fled, leaving me on the urine-splattered tiles, surrounded by nine books, the halves of my peanut butter and jelly sandwich, and my favorite ballpoint pen, somehow snapped in two.

SACRAMENTS OF RECONCILIATION

*T*hey were speeding along the expressway when he noticed something strange: She suddenly pulled her seat belt across her body and clicked it into place. *Now* what is this crazy woman up to, he wondered, and a horrible thought crossed his mind a second before she grabbed and yanked the steering wheel, sending his car through a guardrail and ten feet into the air. As Jimmy and his new girlfriend tumbled toward the earth, my new girlfriend and I lay in his bed, snuggling beneath a warm comforter. More evidence, some might say, that I was the lucky twin.

The first evidence came when we were two. Our mother had just put us to bed and given us strict instructions to stay put. As soon as she left the room, we got up to inspect the riotous noises coming through our second-floor window. A bunch of kids were arguing over a toy. To see better, I leaned hard against the screen, which gave way and landed twenty feet below in the dirt, a second before me. At the hospital I was given a variety of scans and X rays, but the only injury doctors could find was a small scrape on my left elbow, caused when I brushed against the brick wall during my descent.

Five years later Jimmy fell two feet from a swing and broke his arm. Within days of the cast being removed, he toppled off the swings a second time, breaking his arm again.

The following year, when we were eight, I developed a talent for reciting poems. Jimmy developed a stutter. My parents hoped it was a phase but it got worse over time. I remember us sitting in class one day when our fifth-grade teacher asked who wanted to recite Gwendolyn Brooks's poem "We Real Cool." She scanned the room for takers. Five hands inched up, joining the one being swung wildly by a girl who always smelled of pickles. I hoped the teacher would call her. Anyone besides Jimmy. She called Jimmy. He looked up from his desk. The students sitting in front of us turned in their seats, already giggling. The teacher called Jimmy again. I was sitting directly to his right, close enough to see the rapid heaving of his chest, the tremor of his legs. "James," she said once more, "whenever you're ready."

"We . . . We . . . We . . ."

A few students cupped their mouths to hold in the laughter.

"We . . . real . . . *real* . . . *real* . . ."

The teacher huffed.

"Coo . . . coo . . . coo . . . *coo* . . . *coo* . . ."

The teacher said, "Get it *out,* James, for Christ's sake. *Speak!*"

But his throat had fully constricted by then. All he could do at that point was contort his face and gag. Our classmates laughed openly. The teacher shook her head while the pickle-smelling girl continued to wave. I lowered my gaze. The teacher said my name. I rose, recited the poem, and sat back down. When the teacher smiled and declared my recitation perfect, I was seized with a mixture of guilt and pity, as I had been since the third grade, when the onset of Jimmy's stuttering became theater for our classmates and a key means by which teachers told us apart. Since then we had both tried to talk sparingly in each other's company, unless we were alone, or with immediate members of our family, when his throat magically opened as wide as mine.

I was moved to an honors class in sixth grade. Jimmy was moved to a remedial one. It was our first time being separated at school. For the whole year, whenever my teacher wanted something read or recited, I eagerly waved my hand, like the pickle-smelling girl, and other than being compared to her there seemed to be no penalty for it. Except that there was. But I didn't learn of it until one day in my fourteenth year, when Jimmy was sitting on my chest, pounding his fists into my face. I don't remember what spawned the fight, only that he was yelling, "You think you're better than me! You've *always* thought you're better than me!"

I somehow got us flipped around, and now I was on his chest, pounding my fists into his face. "I *do not*," I yelled back, "think I'm better than you!"

But I did; I understand that now. All of our lives we'd been compared and I'd always come out on top; girls told me I was cuter; boys told me I was more fun; teachers said I was smarter; and, as I kicked his ass that day, it seemed I was the better fighter too. But I didn't want to be better than him at anything; I just wanted to be different, to have an identity other than as one of the twins. And so when people began noting my pros and his cons, I internalized them. So did he. We stopped spending time together, unless it was to get high. There'd always be mutual friends around, though, who would separate us when our banter turned to taunts, taunts turned to threats, and threats turned to blows. Only sometimes our friends left too soon, and things got ugly.

One of those occasions ended with me banging his head on the floor until he was unconscious. Another occasion had him chasing me through the neighborhood with a baseball bat and the police looking for us both. They found him first and, at my exasperated parents' urging, took him into custody until he cooled off. Ninety minutes later, when they brought him home, after he'd apologized and expressed contrition, he broke through the barricade of my bedroom door and flung himself at me with a crazed rebel yell. By the time our father pulled him away, he'd bitten off a chunk of my thigh.

"That's *insane*," Brenda said when I showed her the scar, still visible twelve years later.

I laughed and said, "It's nothing. We were just kids. Besides, we were so high all the time then, I mean, everything was just so messed up. It's one of my biggest regrets," I continued, "the way things were between Jimmy and me. We weren't exactly what you'd call close."

"It's not too late to fix that."

I should have said that it probably was too late, but it was still early in our relationship; I wanted to make a good impression. "You're absolutely right," I told her. "And I *will* fix it."

And so that was the response she reminded me of several months later when I declined to visit Jimmy's apartment to celebrate our twenty-eighth birthday. "Everyone's here," he'd said when I called, although that wasn't exactly true. Missing was Zack, who was in prison for burglary; Steve, who was in prison for manslaughter; and Greg, who was dead. Just Tim, Paul, Rob, and Louis were there, and Louis was there in body only, because he hadn't been the same since killing a woman while driving drunk.

If Brenda convinced me to go, I would be there in body only, too. That world was no longer mine, that company no longer the kind I kept, now that I was a college student at the University of Iowa. I was in Chicago for the weekend only to visit Brenda, whom I'd been dating for about eight months. For weeks I'd been looking forward to spending my birthday quietly with her, and now she wanted me to spend it with my twin. As soon as I'd refused his invitation and hung up the phone, she'd said, "Remember when you told me you wanted to fix your relationship with Jimmy?"

"I told you no such thing," I said.

"Of course you did," she responded. "We have to go to his party. He's your *twin*," she reminded me. "Besides, I want to meet him and your friends."

"You don't want to do that," I told her.

"Yes I do. It'll be fun!" she said cheerily. "Come on, *Jerald*."

Everyone else I knew called me Jerry. But Jerry, she'd told me when we'd met, was the name of a child rather than a man. I liked that, how the switch of a name could bring maturity and signify a break with the past. I didn't care much about the maturity part, but breaking with the past was important to me. It was that break I intended to honor now. I was trying to think of an excuse not to go to Jimmy's when she went to her refrigerator and took out a cake.

"What the hell is that?" I asked.

"It's a cake I made," she said.

I laughed.

"What's so funny?"

"It's just, well, these are not exactly cake-eating people."

"*What?* Everybody eats cake." She set it on the table. Then she lifted the receiver off the phone and held it toward me. "Call your twin back," she said.

Thirty minutes later we left her apartment and went downstairs to Jimmy's waiting car. I got in the passenger seat, and Brenda sat behind me. After I introduced Jimmy to her, he pointed toward the cake on her lap. "What the hell is that?" he asked.

"It's a cake!" Brenda said.

Jimmy laughed. Then he took a swallow of his forty-ounce and eased away from the curb.

The stereo was turned up full-blast and the air smelled of cigarettes, marijuana, fish, and rancid oil. Brenda was in the living room, trying to learn how to play bid whist, while Jimmy hovered over the stove, pulling chunks of perch from the bubbling black liquid. I'd just walked in to get another beer. "Hey, bro'," he said, "want some coke?"

I shook my head no. I opened the refrigerator.

"Come on, man," he said. "It's our birthday."

"The beer's cool," I said.

"So you like them Iowa boys now?" he said, laughing. "You just eat corn and go to school and shit? And *bowl*?"

I forced a smile.

"Come on, Jerry. I mean *Jerald*." He burst into laughter, just as the others had done every time Brenda said my name. He put a fresh batch of battered fish into the grease, causing it to roar. "One little hit, for old times' sake," he said. He wiped his hands on his apron, then reached inside his top pocket and took out a small piece of paper. He held it out to me. I glanced into the living room; Brenda was staring at her cards while Rob leaned over her shoulder, telling her something that brought a wrinkle to her brow. I turned back to Jimmy. He was still extending the coke. I took it and backed out of Brenda's view. He handed me a dollar bill, already rolled. I took one small hit, but I wasn't getting high, I told myself, so much as taking a sacrament of reconciliation.

At 2:00 AM the party started to break up. As we were saying our good-byes, Brenda exclaimed, "Wait, wait, I almost forgot!" She ran into the kitchen and returned with the cake. Ignoring the laughter, she sang "Happy Birthday."

Brenda and I ultimately decided to spend the night at Jimmy's and in the morning have him drop her off at her apartment and me at the Greyhound station. He offered us his room before carrying a pillow and spare blankets to the couch. After Brenda and I got in bed, she apologized for the cake, which hadn't turned out the way she'd hoped. "But," she added, "it was kind of everyone to try some."

"They didn't have to spit it out, though. I mean, they could have *swallowed* it. I swallowed some."

"You're sweet," she said. "Everyone was sweet. Especially Jimmy. I didn't know he stuttered, though."

"A little," I said. "It used to be a lot worse."

She snuggled against me, and the next thing I knew I was

being awakened by a ringing phone. I looked at the clock on the nightstand. It was 3:15. The phone rang some more, and I wondered who would be calling at that time and why Jimmy didn't answer it. Finally it stopped. A second later it started again. Brenda was awake now too; she'd pushed herself up on her elbows. "Somebody keeps calling," I grumbled, "and Jimmy's not answering. He had a lot to drink, so he's probably out cold." The ringing stopped. Brenda laid her head back on the pillow. The ringing started once more.

Brenda sat up again. "Maybe you should answer it," she said. "Maybe it's an emergency."

I dismissed that possibility, but only long enough for the ringing to pause and resume. I climbed out of bed and went into the kitchen, where the phone was mounted on the wall.

"Hello?"

"Jerry?"

"Yes? Who's this?"

"Jimmy's been in a terrible car accident."

"Mom?"

"Jimmy's been in a crash . . ."

"Mom, what are you *talking* about? Jimmy's asleep on the couch."

I felt a draft of cold air coming from my right. I glanced in that direction and saw that the kitchen door was wide open. My mother was saying something as I set the phone on the counter and hurried into the living room. The couch was empty, the blankets in a heap on the floor. I went back to the phone. *"What happened?"*

"What . . . aren't you listening?"

"What happened?" I asked again. Brenda was standing next to me now, wrapped in the comforter.

"Jimmy was in a terrible crash."

"Where is he?" I yelled.

"Cook County Hospital."

I hung up. I told Brenda what I knew and we hurried to get dressed. Except there was a problem: Buses didn't start running until dawn, and there were no taxis in that part of the city after dark, and rarely during the day. We put on our coats, left the apartment, and started walking.

Three hours later, just as the sun was beginning to rise, we walked through the emergency room doors. The receptionist offered no information on Jimmy's condition, only that he was about to go to surgery. She told us where he was.

We found him in a hall, lying in a long row of gurneys covered with patients moaning and calling for help. His face was bruised and swollen, but he was conscious. As soon as he saw us, he tried to speak. "My . . . my . . . my . . . ," he began, and suddenly we were back in the fifth grade. "They're . . . ta . . . ta . . . taking . . . *my . . . my . . . arm.*" I looked at Brenda. Her hand was over her mouth, like our classmates, only she wasn't laughing. I started to reach for Jimmy but I didn't know where it was safe to touch, so I just stood there, not knowing what to say or do, until an orderly wheeled him away.

I went to call my parents and they gave me the rest of the story. Jimmy's girlfriend had walked away from the crash, leaving him lying in the street, his right arm trapped beneath the hood of the upended car. He hadn't been wearing his seat belt. The doctors said he should have died.

Four hours later, when the surgeon came to talk to us, he stressed that point. "How he survived," he said, "is beyond me." They'd managed to save his arm, though only time would tell how much function it would regain.

Soon after the surgeon left, the double doors of the operating room parted and Jimmy was wheeled through. He was unconscious, with only his bandaged head and IV'ed left arm exposed from the bundle of blankets. Brenda and I followed the orderly as he steered him into a large room filled with a few dozen other patients. Jimmy's bed was parked in an empty slot near a window and four folding chairs. Brenda and I sat and waited for him to wake. It took an hour. I saw his eyes flutter open, and then they filled with terror as he began clawing frantically at his blankets, yanking off layer after layer. I went to his side. And if I could have spoken at that moment, I would have told him that everything was okay, that his arm was still there, that he was lucky to be alive.

BADDEST NIGGER IN TOWN

When she led me through the living room, I was startled by a cage of agitated finches. There weren't any finches the last time I was there. I was eleven then and selling cookies for my church. Her father had invited me in. While making change for a twenty, I'd eased onto the arm of the sofa and before I realized my mistake I was being roughly ushered from the house. "And don't come back," her father snapped, "until you can treat my property with respect!" That night, I hurled a rock through one of the windows, and now, four years later, I was standing at the very spot where the glass had littered the floor, removing my pants.

"Is this your room?" I asked.

She shook her head. "My parents'."

"And they won't be back for two hours?"

"Maybe longer."

I took off my shirt. Jean was undressing, too, though she did so beneath the pastel blanket of her parents' bed. It was a large bed and had an expensive brass headboard that was good for securing handcuffs. She'd found the handcuffs a few months before, when she'd also found adult toys, satin lingerie, *Playboy* magazines, some yellow pills in an unmarked box, and a stack of dirty movies. "Want to watch a dirty movie?" she asked, giggling.

"Sure," I said, now undressed to my briefs and feeling self-conscious about my physique. I was very skinny, despite all the protein shakes I'd choked down and the fifty push-ups I did every night. But it was losing your virginity that would trigger a boy's growth; Tim had told me so. I'd been wanting to test this hypothesis with Jean for two weeks, after she'd slipped me her phone number during our history class. I'd called her many times since then, my rambling, awkward efforts growing eloquent and witty when I'd had a little wine. I'd had a little wine when I begged her to have sex with me. She'd invited me over.

"Look in there." She giggled again and pointed toward the closet. "To the right. There's a chest full of movies and a projector."

I did as I was told and found a movie with a hilarious title, something like *Baddest Nigger in Town*. We laughed when I read that aloud. I read a few more funny titles, we laughed some more, and then I settled on one that was blank. I set up the projector and snapped on the reel. I flicked on the power. A square of white covered the wall when the reel began to churn. I inhaled a whiff of burning dust as I turned and faced Jean. The blanket was up to her chin. On the floor next to the bed were a skirt, a blouse, panties, and a training bra. I stepped over them as I went to sit next to her. After swinging my lower half beneath the covers, I slid my underwear off and dropped it with her things. The wall began to fill with naked bodies. Her hand crept up my thigh. "What's wrong?" she asked.

For a second I was too mortified to respond. "I don't know."

She removed her hand. "Let's just watch the movie," she suggested.

We did for a while and then I stammered, "I'm not . . . I'm not a sissy."

"What?"

"I'm not a sissy."

"I didn't say you are."

"Don't even *think* it."

"I'm not *thinking* it." She was silent for a moment before adding, "You're just nervous."

But that was unacceptable too.

BOBBY JENKINS

*E*rica was born and raised in a poor white community where blacks were a rare and unwelcome sight. When I visited for the first and only time, it was at a barbecue in the backyard of one of her cousins, and throughout the day relatives dropped by to see the source of the scandal in person. It was an awkward, tension-filled event, though incident-free, except for when one of Erica's brothers approached me while extending a can of Brazil nuts and said, "Help yourself to some more nigger toes." He laughed; so I laughed and took a few. He patted me on the back before driving me to his apartment where, while we drank a case of beer, he showed me video after video of white women having sex with animals. Every once in a while, he'd grin at me and say, "Ain't this some *sick* shit?" I would agree. Later, I would wonder if he'd been trying to make a point, but at the time I was too horrified to care.

My welcoming into Brenda's family was different, though not necessarily better.

She has four half siblings, all born to her father and his first wife. When their marriage failed, she left him with two of the children, an uncommon occurrence in a culture where child rearing was strictly the mother's domain. Perhaps Brenda's mother found his role as struggling single father endearing, or maybe she'd been taken in by his charm, grace, and soft-spoken manner.

And then there were his good looks, a Sidney Poitier in his prime. Whatever the appeal, it must have been quite the shock to her when, two months after they'd met, just a few days after their wedding, he beat her.

Almost immediately she began plotting her escape back to the States, except that she had no money, and she wasn't sure where she would go. She too had been born in a poor white community, just a short drive from Erica's, and her family had disowned her when she wrote to say that the man she'd married was not only black but one of the originals, an *African,* the lowest form of human existence, in her family's view, on Planet Earth. It was this kind of small-mindedness that had suffocated her since her earliest memories and made her yearn to live in a distant land, a place whose quaint, exotic culture would help her forget the sinful flaws of her own. After college, she taught elementary school for a few years before departing for Africa, settling into life as an educator and expatriate in a rural Zambian village, relieved to be free of her intolerant family, of American racism, of the belief that blacks and whites could not live together in peace and harmony, only to find herself being assaulted by her black husband and, three months after their marriage, expecting his child.

Brenda was born in 1969. She was eight weeks premature, weighed just four pounds, and was not expected to live. Doctors kept her in the hospital for a month, trying to regulate her body temperature with the best medical technology available—an insulated cardboard box and an eighty-watt lightbulb. By some miracle she survived, and by another miracle Brenda's mother managed to secretly stash away a little money each month, so that in three years' time she had enough to fly herself and her daughter to the States. But here the miracles ceased; on the eve of her departure, her husband found the passport she'd gotten, which included Brenda's name. The beating he gave her might have been fatal had he not decided that she could go after all, because that way he could go too. And of course, they would take his eleven- and twelve-year-old children, Judy and Robert. It would be Robert who, two decades later, would call me frequently in my Iowa City hippie commune, sometimes well after midnight, and tell me he was going to kick my ass.

"Why?" I asked him the first time.

"You know why."

"Actually, I don't."

"You *know*."

This was the spring of 1992, around March or April. Brenda and I had been dating for almost a year. She still lived in Chicago, but not for much longer; she had been accepted into the master's program in art history at the University of Iowa. Robert had not been happy when he learned she would be leaving town, but not unhappy enough to harass me. That started when she told him we would be cohabitating.

"You and me," he continued, "we need to sit down and talk."

"Okay," I said. "I'm looking forward to it. Brenda has told me a lot about you."

"Did she tell you I can bench-press three hundred pounds?"

"No, she neglected to mention that."

"How about squats? Did she mention the size of my quads? They're *mammoth*."

I suddenly realized he was drunk. Brenda confirmed with me the next day that he did have trouble in that regard. She insisted too that he was harmless, a typical overprotective big brother who, once I got to know him, would become my close friend. But we were off to a bad start. And his nighttime calls continued for several months. By the eighth or ninth call, my inner thug had been awakened.

"Actually," I responded to him one night, "I'm going to kick *your* ass."

"Oh, yeah?"

"Yeah!"

"*Yeah?*"

"*Yeah!*"

We met for the first time that summer. There was no ass-kicking, no bestiality movies, just a man-to-man drive through the winding streets of Elk Grove Village during which he spoke of how much he loved his baby sister. I assured him I loved her too. "I'll treat her well," I told him.

"If you don't," he said, "expect a thorough ass-kicking."

"Oh, yeah?"

"Yeah!"

"Oh, *yeah?*"

"*Yeah!*"

I let it go. He parked the car and hugged me.

Judy and I hit it off right from the start, too well, in fact, for her husband Craig's taste. He was white, tall, thin, muscular, blond, and blue-eyed, a recipe for self-confidence that was undermined by his lack of education, wit, personality, or patience for a wife who liked to flirt and wear skirts that proved mammoth thighs ran in the family. She and I had a tremendous amount of fun when we were together, and after Brenda graduated from UIC and moved to Iowa City, Judy would often call just to speak to me. Whenever we visited her, Judy and I would plant ourselves on the couch and laugh and joke for long periods while Craig fumed nearby. One day he decided enough was enough. I don't know exactly what he told her, but an hour after we left her house and stopped by her mother's condominium, Judy called, asked to speak with me, and yelled into the receiver, "How dare you insult Craig like that, you . . . you . . . you *common street nigger!*"

"That was odd," I said, after hanging up the phone and sitting back at the table, where Brenda, her mother, and I were having dinner.

Brenda looked up from her plate. "What was odd?"

"Judy. She called me a common street nigger."

A bit of food sprayed from Brenda's mouth, landing on my sleeve. "*What?*"

"Just now."

"*Why?*"

"Not sure. Something about my having insulted Craig."

We both faced her mother. She was quietly humming a song while slicing a piece of meat from a chicken leg.

"*Mom,*" Brenda began, "aren't you going to *do* something?"

She looked up. "What do you want me to do?"

"Well, call Judy back and tell her that's unacceptable! Make her apologize!"

"Why should I?" she asked, now facing me. "We're all entitled to our opinions."

It was not the response I wanted, but it was the kind of response I'd come to expect. Her opinion of men in general was low, thanks to her husband, from whom she was separated, and her opinion of me was even lower, thanks to my delinquent past. I hadn't mentioned this past to her; to the contrary, I presented myself in the most positive light I could muster, going so far as to abandon my hippie clothes, shave my sideburns and goatee, and remove one of my two earrings. During the first year after we'd met, I'd mailed her silly Hallmark cards for her birthday and all the major holidays, and I went out of my way to compliment her cooking and her hair. She'd responded to these friendly overtures with indifference. Finally, as Brenda and I approached our second year of being together, I made a last-ditch effort to win her affection by showing her some of my writing. Perhaps, my reasoning went, she'd see a glimmer of talent and conclude that I wasn't a total loser.

"What's this?" she asked when I handed her a short story.

We were in the living room of Brenda's and my Iowa City apartment, where her mother had come to visit for a few days. She had just unpacked her things and was relaxing on the couch. I sat next to her. "Oh, just a little something I wrote," I said. "I'm thinking of submitting it to the Iowa Writers' Workshop next month with my application."

"Should I read it?" she asked.

"If you don't mind."

She smiled. "I don't mind at all," she said, drawing the manuscript closer to her face. Brenda came into the room with a bowl of popcorn and sat in a chair across from us. She turned on the TV, and she and I watched the evening news until I saw her mother lower my story to her lap.

"So," I asked, "what did you think?"

"I think," she said, "that you are a criminal, and that you should be ashamed of yourself for the awful things you've done."

I shot a look at Brenda and then back at her mother. "That wasn't *me* in the story," I said. "It's fiction."

She snickered. "It's you."

"Mom," Brenda interjected. "It's *fiction*. Just because Jerald wrote it doesn't mean it's about him."

"Except," she said, "that it obviously is."

"It's *not* me," I insisted. "It's about a fictitious character named Bobby Jenkins. I made him up."

"Of course you did," she said.

I recall being extremely upset by this exchange, not solely because she had drawn conclusions about me based on my story, but because she had tapped into my growing fear that no matter how educated I became, no matter how sober, or how law-abiding and clean-shaven, people would always see me not as the person I'd become, but rather as the person I used to be—the embodiment of the stereotypical black thug that pervades the American psyche. But the thing about it was that sometimes, when my self-esteem was low, I still saw myself that way too. And maybe, in some ways, that wasn't such a bad thing. Because being a thug meant I possessed a certain toughness, a kind of *fuck you* attitude that allowed me to laugh when offered a can of nuts as black toes, or to brush it off when called a common street nigger, or to not want the love and acceptance of my girlfriend's mother. "You know what," I'd begun after she refused to chastise Judy, but I held my tongue. Her opinion of me, I told myself, simply didn't matter.

But it did. And I realized just how much a week later, after Brenda and I had returned to Iowa City. I'd finished classes for the day and was on my way to see the graduate dean, James Jakobsen, whom I'd gotten to know well over the years because of his work with minority students. As soon as I walked into his office, he said, "Hey, I was just talking about you."

"Really?" I sat in the chair in front of his desk. "What's up?" I asked, digging in my backpack for my turkey sandwich.

"The Writers' Workshop just called," he said. "They're looking for funding for you."

"Funding? For what?"

"Don't you get it?" he said, grinning. He rose and joined me on the other side of the desk. "You've been *accepted* into the program. One of only twenty-three, I think, out of about eight hundred applicants this year." He extended his hand for a shake. "Boy, that's something, Jerald. That's really something."

The next few seconds are lost to me forever. All I remember is running at full sprint across the campus, heading toward the union, where Brenda and some of her fellow art history students often had lunch. It was a little before noon, and when I burst through the doors of the cafeteria, it was so crowded that, if she was there, I doubted I'd ever find her. I moved in and out of the bodies and tables like a mouse in a maze, and as I was about to give up I heard Brenda call my name. I turned to my left and saw her; she was standing near a table in the far corner of the room, waving me over. I began working my way through the throng of bodies, nearly knocking a few down, already yelling my news so that many people in the room knew of my good fortune long before Brenda and I embraced. For the next several seconds, we just stood there holding each other, both of us crying, Brenda pulling back at some point to say how proud she was of me, and I, for a fleeting instant, longed to hear those words from her mother.

THE SOULS OF WHITE FOLK

*T*he white boys had no game but the refs were on their side. That's because the refs were white, too. So were the hundreds of people in the stands. So was probably every person in this exclusive Chicago suburb that had castles as houses and parks for lawns. By the second quarter it was clear that we would lose, ending our shot at being regional champions. That this was happening in our church league would have made matters worse, except for the fact that by then I knew God was white as well. So rather than getting angry like our coaches and frustrated like my teammates, I relaxed on the bench next to Jimmy, both of us casually sipping from our water bottles, which we'd filled with gin and juice.

When halftime finally arrived, we were down by two dozen points, which wasn't bad, considering the extent of our opposition. The two teams filed into separate locker rooms. As soon as we had gathered around our coach, one of the boys said, "The referees are cheating."

"And that short kid," someone else said, "called me a nigger."

"Me too!" another boy added.

And then a fourth boy looked at our coach and asked, "Why are they doing this? I mean, aren't these things, you know, sins?"

"They're doing this," the coach snapped, "because these are some racist honkies."

I gagged, sending gin and juice all over my pristine jersey. I stared at our coach, shocked, and yet relieved that he was calling it like it was. I wanted to hear him say it again. "What did you say?" I asked.

But he wouldn't repeat it. Instead he paced in front of us, lost in thought with his finger over his lips, as if to shush himself. He paused next to me and exhaled a stream of air that smelled like the pipe he smoked. I took another sip of my drink.

"Young men," he began, his voice low and measured, "it's time you learned that even God's chosen ones are not entirely without sin. We are all flawed in the eyes of the Lord—some of us more so than others. We know that what is happening is sinful. We know that these actions are wrong. Therefore, it is our responsibility," he continued, and I got the sense he was trying to convince himself of what he was about to say, "it is our obligation to pray for the souls of these white folk, for they know not what they do." He bowed his head and led us in prayer. When he finished, he told us to take a few minutes to contemplate what he'd said, and then he left, the two assistant coaches on his heels.

Michael, our center, broke the silence. "What the coach just said," he began, "was some A-1 bullshit." Jimmy and I liked Michael. His family had joined the church only six months earlier, and he was decidedly not receptive to its teachings. He had gin and juice in his water bottle too. "These white folks know what the hell they're doing all right. That's why they're doing it! And I don't know about you all, but the next time one of these honkies gets the ball near me, I'm letting him have it!" To emphasize *have it,* Michael kicked one of the lockers, causing the flimsy wire to give way and his foot to disappear inside. He threw his hands over his mouth and mumbled, "Oh, shit," and then, as he removed his foot, his eyes grew large. He bent over, reached inside the locker, and pulled out a brand-new pair of leather Converse All Stars. We all watched quietly as he sat on a bench and took off his shoes—which, like the rest of ours, were canvas and spotted with small holes. He slipped on the left All Star, and then the right. After he'd tied the strings he rose and walked a few feet away, lowered himself into a deep knee bend, and then sprang himself high in the air. He turned to face us as he looked toward the heavens. "Forgive me, Lord," he said, "for I know not what I do either."

The rest of us started kicking in lockers.

WORKSHOPPED

When I was in my early twenties and making my first crude attempts at writing fiction, I'd sit at my word processor and pound out stories brimming with blacks who understood only anger and pain. My settings were always ghettos, because that was what I knew, and the plots centered on hardship and suffering, because I knew that, too. And I also knew this: White society was responsible for the existence of this miserable world, and it was my duty as a black artist to make this clear. Three of these stories were what had gained me acceptance into the Iowa Writers' Workshop. It was there that my awakening occurred.

My first course was with Frank Conroy, the program's director. He was brutally honest and harbored a militant obsession with clarity. Most of the two-hour classes were spent with him shredding the stories and our egos. We squirmed in our seats and wiped our brows as he did his infamous line-by-line, zeroing in on words and phrases that confused the work's meaning or failed to make unequivocal sense. It was the most intense and best writing class that I'd ever had. I went into the second semester confident that my prose had improved and that the most difficult course was behind me.

Randomly, I decided to take a workshop with James Alan McPherson. During the break before classes resumed, I read for the first time his books *Hue and Cry* and *Elbow Room*. The impact his writing had on me was profound. He, too, chronicled the lives of African Americans, and he had done it in short-story form, at the time my genre of choice; this was the model I'd been searching for. I read the stories over and over again, convinced that I had found my literary father.

The contrast between Conroy and McPherson could not have been more stark. Conroy was tall, white, and boisterous; McPherson was short, black, and shy. Conroy cursed, yelled, laughed, and joked; McPherson rarely spoke at all, and when he did his voice was so quiet you often couldn't hear him. The students dominated his workshops. I was disappointed. McPherson was a Pulitzer Prize winner, after all, the first African American to receive that honor for fiction. He was the recipient of a MacArthur "genius" grant and countless other awards. I wanted his wisdom. I wanted his insight. He gave it midsemester, when it was time to workshop my first story.

"Before we begin today," he said, "I'd like to make a few comments." This was new; he'd never prefaced a story before. A smile crept on my face as I allowed myself to imagine him praising me for my depiction of a den of heroin addicts, for this was not easy to do, requiring, among other things, an intimate knowledge of heroin addicts and a certain flair for profanity.

"Are you all familiar with gangsta rap?" McPherson asked. We were, despite the fact that, besides me, all of the students were white and mostly middle to upper class. While we each nodded our familiarity with the genre, McPherson reached into a shopping bag he'd brought and removed a magazine. He opened it to a premarked page on which was a picture of a rapper, cloaked in jewelry and guns and leaning against the hood of a squad car. Behind him was a sprawling slum. "This person raps about the ghetto," McPherson said, "but he doesn't live in the ghetto. He lives in a wealthy white suburb with his wife and daughter. His daughter attends a predominantly white private school. That's what this article is about." He closed the magazine and returned it to the bag. "What some gangsta rappers are doing is using black stereotypes because white people eat that stuff up. But these images are false, they're dishonest. Some rappers are selling out their race for personal gain." He paused again, this time to hold up my story. "That's what this writer is doing with his work." He sat my story back on the table. "Okay, that's all I have to say. You can discuss it now."

For a few seconds, the only sound in the room was my labored breathing. And then someone said, "McPherson's right. The story is garbage."

"Complete rubbish," said another.

And so it went from there.

I did not sleep that night. At 8:00 AM, when I could hold out no longer, I called McPherson at home and demanded a conference. He agreed to meet me in his office in ten minutes.

He was there when I arrived, sitting behind his desk. The desk was bare except for a copy of my story, and the office was bare except for the desk and two chairs. The built-in bookshelves held nothing, and nothing hung on the walls. There was no dressing on the window, no telephone, and no computer. It might have been the janitor's office, a place to catch a few winks while the mopped floors dried. And McPherson might have been the janitor. His blue shirt was a mass of wrinkles and his eyes were bloodshot. His trademark hat, a beige straw Kangol, seemed to rest at an odd angle on his head; from beneath it a single long braid had worked its way free and dangled rebelliously behind his right ear. He noticed me staring at it and poked it back into concealment.

"Are you okay?" he asked. His voice was gentle, full of concern. "You sounded like a crazy man on the phone."

"Well, I'm *not* a crazy man." I reached forward to tap my finger on my story and proceeded to rant and rave as only a crazy man could. "I did not make this stuff up," I insisted. "I'm *from* the ghetto." I went through the characters one by one, citing various relatives on whom they were based, and I mentioned that, just the week before, my younger brother had been shot in the back while in McDonald's. I told him I had another brother who was in and out of prison, a heroin-addict sister-in-law, that I had once been arrested for car theft (falsely, but that was beside the point), and that many, many of my friends were presently still living in the miserable community in which I'd been raised. "You misread my story," I said in conclusion, "and you misread *me*." I leaned back and folded my arms across my chest, waiting for his apology. Instead, I watched as he sprang from his chair and hurried from the room. He turned left into the hall, and a moment later he passed going right, with Frank Conroy calling after him, and then they passed left again, now with Connie Brothers, the program's administrator, in tow, and after two more passes this awful parade came to an end somewhere out of view. Then Connie stood before me, looking as nauseated as I felt. "Jim is the kindest soul on this earth," she said quietly. "Why, why would you insult him?"

For an instant I saw myself at fourteen, looking at a closed front door, behind which was my first love, who had just dumped me and left me standing on her porch trying unsuccessfully not to cry.

Connie magically produced a tissue and handed it to me. She rubbed my shoulders while I rambled incoherently, something about sleep deprivation and McPherson being my father. "It's okay, sweetie," Connie said. "I'll talk to him."

McPherson returned momentarily. I apologized. He told me it was okay, that workshops can make people uptight and sensitive. It had been difficult for him too, he explained, when he was a student there in the 1970s. There was a lull in the conversation before he said, "So, where're your people from?"

He still doesn't believe me, I thought. I mumbled, "Chicago."

"No, no. That's where they *are*. Where are they *from*?"

"Oh, sorry. Arkansas."

"Mine are from Georgia," he said. He smiled and added, "That place is a *motherfucker*."

The essence of black America was conveyed in that response, a toughness of spirit, humor laced with tragedy, but at that moment all I saw was the man who had rejected my vision. Defeated, I thanked him for agreeing to meet with me as I rose to leave. He stood and shook my hand. As I was walking out the door, he called my name. I turned to face him.

"Stereotypes are valuable," he said. "But *only* if you use them to your advantage. They present your readers with something they'll recognize, and it pulls them into what appears to be familiar territory, a comfort zone. But once they're in, you have to move them beyond the stereotype. You have to show them what's real."

"What's real?" I asked.

Without hesitation he said, "You."

It was one of those things that you instantly recognize as profound, and then, because you don't quite understand it, try to forget as quickly as you can. It was also one of those things that you cannot forget. And so it roamed freely in my subconscious, occasionally coming into sharp focus to remind me of its presence, but I allowed myself to be consumed by it no more than I would a housefly. For about a year. And then I went to see him again.

"I was wondering," I said, "if you wouldn't mind supervising an independent project."

"That depends," he responded, "on what you'd like to study."

"Me," I said. "I want to study me."

We started with black folklore and history. Next we moved on to blues and jazz, and then we covered a broad range of black literature and culture. We studied black intellectuals and philosophers, sociologists, and anthropologists, activists, filmmakers, and ex-cons. We dissected nearly every aspect of black life and thought, and in the process a theme emerged that had been there all along: *Life* is a motherfucker; living it anyway, and sometimes laughing in the process, is where humanity is won.

And this is what I learned about me: I had become my own stereotype, a character in one of my short stories who insisted on seeing himself primarily as a repository of pain and defeat, despite overwhelming evidence to the contrary. The very people with whom I had been raised and whom I had dedicated myself to rendering in prose had become victims of my myopia. My stories showed people being affected by drug addiction, racism, poverty, murder, crime, violence, but they said nothing about the spirit that, despite being confronted with what often amounted to certain defeat, would continue to struggle and aspire for something better.

That old slave song "We Shall Overcome" pretty much says it all.

BAD OUTCOMES

*A*t 10:00 PM the bank's parking lot contained only one car. Six of us were crouched behind it. The bank's rear door was thirty feet away. When it opened, we sprinted toward the hand that waved us in.

Our shoes were damp from snow and squeaked loudly on the lobby's tiles. The shrill noise vanished when we reached the carpeted stairs, replaced by rapid thumps and heavy breathing. The building's warmth had felt pretty good when we'd entered, but by the time we reached the third floor I was hot and sweaty. I pulled off my skullcap and stuffed it inside my parka; then I took off my parka and hung it on a coatrack to my right, near the massive vault. The others had already done the same, and now they pulled chairs from desks and positioned them around the one in the far right corner, which belonged to Tim. Tim sat behind it, lighting a joint. The two bottles of wine we'd brought were already in circulation.

We had been doing this for several months, since one of Tim's professors had landed him a high-paying internship with a local bank. Tim was an accountant, scheduled to work from nine at night to five in the morning, an otherwise lonely assignment had he not regularly invited Jimmy, me, and four of our friends there to keep him company. It was risky behavior, fraught with potentially bad outcomes, such as the forgotten half-smoked joint we'd leave that would get Tim fired and expelled from school. But that wouldn't be for several weeks; for now I was impressed with our audacity, and every now and then I'd pause to marvel at the fact of seven black males in such close proximity to millions of dollars, getting stoned.

At around 1:00 or 2:00 AM we'd leave, the long trip home sobering us enough to sneak back into our homes without waking our parents, though sometimes Jimmy drank too much, making it difficult to get him all the way to our upstairs bedroom.

On one of those early mornings, after I'd gotten Jimmy to our room, I led him to his bed and then collapsed on my own, only to wake a few minutes later to the sound of his vomiting. Linda did too; I sat up to see her standing in our doorway in her pajamas, backlit by the lamp she'd turned on in her room across the hall. "You have to stop this," she pleaded as she sat next to me.

"What?" I grinned, barely suppressing a laugh. "We're just having some fun."

"There'll be plenty of time for fun when you're older. For now you need to focus on school."

I thought of the taunting and the hoodlums, of the courses too easy to hold my interest, and suddenly my substance-induced giddiness was gone. I looked toward the floor and mumbled, "I hate school."

"But that's okay. You just have to get through it."

"I can't get through it."

"Yes you can."

I shook my head. "It's not the right place for me."

"Then think about what is," she said. "Think about the future. Where do you want to be in five years? Where do you see yourself being?"

How could I see myself being somewhere in five years, I wondered, when I couldn't see myself being anywhere now? "You don't understand," I whined, but I didn't really either, so I simply re-peated this phrase over and over, as if doing so would make the understanding come. It didn't. But Linda was patient with me; she waited until I'd worked myself to tears before removing my shoes and tucking me under the covers. And then she went to help Jimmy, who, it must have seemed to her, needed her more.

WE ARE AMERICANS

I was midair, somewhere above the Atlantic, when I stopped being black. I was informed of it two days later. "Now you are colored," I was told.

"What does that mean," I asked, "colored?"

"It means you are not black, like you were in America."

"Am . . . am I . . . *white*?"

"No, but you are very, very close. Close enough that the blacks here will hate you."

Here was Harare, Zimbabwe, where Brenda and I would live for two months while she conducted her dissertation research. Her goal was to document the murals women painted on their homes in the rural areas, but first we had to live in the capital city so she could work in the national archives. During the two days since our arrival, I'd noticed that some of the locals weren't particularly friendly; I'd just asked our hostess Farai about our rude reception. She was surprised that we hadn't been warned, especially by Brenda's father, since this was his native land. Farai was his niece.

"Oh, yes," Farai continued. "Your time here with the blacks will be very, very difficult."

"What about with the whites?" Brenda asked.

Farai smiled. "They will hate you as well, but not as much."

Just like that, I'd been cast in *The Twilight Zone,* in an episode on racial purgatory. Brenda had had experience with this sort of thing, being the child of a mixed marriage, but both my parents were black, certified Negroes from lands of "chitlins" and cotton. I had been black for thirty-one years, and now my caramel complexion and nappy hair had somehow betrayed me. I was stunned, confused beyond measure. Farai offered us some tea.

This was 1995, fifteen years after the start of Zimbabwe's democratic rule. Prior to that, it was an apartheid state. Whites had controlled the country, despite being less than 5 percent of the population, and they'd decided that an even smaller percentage of the population, people of mixed ancestry, the coloreds, should be next in line. Coloreds were provided good schools and housing. They were hired for cushy jobs. They were granted the right to vote. And, according to Farai, they exercised their right to be snide. Now blacks were in power. It was payback time.

"But, but . . . ," I stammered, *"we are Americans."*

"All the worse," Farai responded.

"Why?"

"Blacks hate Americans, too."

"Why?"

"Because Americans are rich."

"Not all of them," I told her, but by comparison this wasn't true. Seventy percent of black Zimbabweans were poor, poor in a way that I had not understood, even though I'd been raised in projects and slums. Harare was full of beggars, more naked than not, smelly, dirty, sick, and occasionally missing limbs. Those who could walk had followed us for long periods with their hands extended, and those who could not tugged at our pant legs or called out to us as we passed. I had made a concerted effort to ignore these things, since the African experience I had envisioned for myself had been entirely uplifting, bordering on the spiritual, much in the way that visiting Mecca had been for Malcolm X. Only better. After all, I, a descendant of African slaves, was returning to the motherland, home of the men and women who had endured the middle passage's horrors to bequeath me their genes. And now I was back to claim my long-denied birthright—a sense of belonging, a sense of place. Just the thought of it had brought me to tears.

And it had brought my sister Linda to tears too. In recent years, she'd become obsessed with her ancestral roots, filling her apartment with items purchased from African art peddlers who traveled through black communities like gypsies, doing brisk business from the trunks of their cars. Her walls held a number of imposing masks, their backs scrawled with the name of a country and an exotic-sounding tribe. Brenda, who was completing her doctorate in African art history, knew instantly that all of the items were fakes, but she didn't have the heart to tell my sister, as I would later not have the heart to tell her that Africa—at least the one of our imaginations—wasn't real either. "And *this* one," Linda would say to us, pointing toward a lopsided wooden head with the teeth of a walrus and the horns of a ram, "was made by the Pee-*ack*-boo of Nigeria." While we nodded thoughtfully, she'd stand there beaming in her mud-cloth gown, leaning on one of her intricately carved canes, the small head of a god snug in the palm of her hand.

A week before we'd left, Linda had thrown a "Back to Africa" party in our honor. She'd spent hours making an "African feast" of fried chicken and catfish, collard greens, neck bones, oxtails, sweet potatoes, and potato salad. Standing at the head of the picnic table, she'd raised her forty-ounce of malt liquor high in the air and spoken passionately of how important it was to maintain our bond with the ancestors, how fortunate I was to be able to take this trip, and how, thanks to me, the severed link with our African kin would soon be restored. And then she tilted the bottle to offer libations, which evoked a gasp from our brother Tim, who staggered drunkenly toward the falling liquid with cupped hands.

I think I cried during her speech. I *know* I cried on the plane.

When our slow descent at last brought the motherland into view, I wiped my eyes and tried to say the words *I'm home* but found I was too emotional to speak. By the time our wheels skipped across the tarmac, I sobbed openly; this, I imagined, was what it felt like for a long-held hostage to at last be freed. And so it was difficult to accept Farai's view that, while I had been away in captivity, the locks on the homeland's doors had been changed.

That night, as Brenda and I lay in bed trying to make sense of all that her cousin had told us, we decided to reject our colored status. We would simply explain, as often as necessary, that Zimbabwe's system of racial classification did not apply to us, that we had always been and would always be black. I fell asleep convinced that this would suffice, and the next morning I woke with so much of my idealism about Africa restored that it would take a full three weeks for it to be thoroughly shattered.

The first crack occurred the next day. After spending six hours at the archives, we were driving home when we came upon a military blockade. There were half a dozen cars ahead of us in the queue, and one by one the officers, unsmiling with rifles strapped over their torsos like guitars, interrogated the occupants and sometimes searched their vehicles. When it was our turn, an officer approached me and barked, "Open the boot!"

I did not know what a boot was or how to open one. "Open the *what?*" I asked.

He did a double take, caused by either my ignorance or my accent. I drew back as he rested his hands on the door and leaned closer, looking from me to Brenda to me again and smelling strongly of tobacco. "Why do you speak this way?" he asked. "Who do you think you are fooling?"

"No . . . no one," I said. "We're Americans."

He grinned. "Ah, but you are a liar! You live in Chitungwiza. I have seen you there myself many times before."

"No, no," I insisted, "we *really* are Americans. It's true!"

"Show me your documentation then, *Mr. America.*"

I retrieved my passport from my backpack and handed it to him. He looked at it only briefly before saying, "But this is not you. This is a *white* man."

It was, I admit, an unflattering picture. The flash of the camera had bathed my face in light, making me appear even paler than had Iowa's overcast winter. Moreover, hours of intense Zimbabwean sun had given me a rich tan. The guard's confusion was understandable. "I'm not white," I politely explained. "I'm not colored either, actually. I'm black."

He exploded in violent laughter. He waved the other officers over and showed them my passport. "This man says he is *black*," he told them, and while the others laughed he composed himself enough to light a cigarette. Smoke puffed from his mouth as he demanded more documentation. I gave him my driver's license. He held it close to his face. The other men peered over his shoulders, all eyes darting between the two pictures and me. After a short debate in Shona, I was handed my identification. The officers stepped back from the car, and the one who had stopped me, frowning now, waved me forward with the barrel of his rifle.

"This sucks," I said as we drove away.

"Yes, it does," Brenda agreed. "And now you know what it's like to be me. Sometimes I'm white, sometimes I'm black, sometimes I'm both, sometimes I'm neither. I've also been Indian, Pakistani, and Moroccan." She laughed devilishly, clearly enjoying my indoctrination into her strange world of racial schizophrenia. It *was* kind of funny, I had to confess, and soon I was laughing too.

For a while, it was our laughter that sustained us. We laughed when we were ignored in restaurants and retail stores; we laughed when pedestrians deliberately bumped into us; we laughed when we arrived at the hotels of tourist sites and were told that we had no reservations. For two weeks we laughed at every slight and insult that came our way, and we might have laughed for the rest of our trip had we not made the mistake one afternoon of ordering ice cream at an outdoor café, right in the heart of Harare.

We'd just started eating our sundaes when two boys sat at our table. Shocked by their boldness, Brenda and I looked around, hoping one of the employees would chase them off, but no one paid us any attention. We tried ignoring our uninvited guests, as we had ignored countless other beggars, but the stench radiating from them was magnetic, pulling our gaze to its source. They could not have been older than ten. Neither one had a shirt or shoes; their skin was covered with open sores. Things moved in their hair. The boys said nothing, understanding, perhaps, that there was nothing to say. They were starving. We were not. They were poor. We were rich. They felt wronged. We felt guilty. We gave them our sundaes. It helped none of us very much.

Sometimes we'd be driving and see on the roadside women and small children selling tomatoes. We'd stop and buy them all. We bought things obsessively, loaves of bread from old men on bicycles, potatoes from little girls who pulled them in wagons, and, from street vendors, dozens of knickknacks carved in stone. But that didn't help either. In the end, to save ourselves, we learned to look through our guilt, as if it were no more than a dirty window, and concentrate on pleasant things in the distance. We let ourselves be colored.

We started patronizing businesses staffed by whites because whites treated us better. We sought out white convenience stores, white malls, white gas stations. We preferred the company of whites when we should have despised it. Once, while eating in a white restaurant, the waiter asked where we were headed. We mentioned a certain park we'd heard was nice. "Oh, *don't* go there," he warned us. "It's overrun by blacks." We did not go.

The friendliest white person we met there wasn't from there at all. He was from Tyler, Texas, on safari with his family. He approached us while we were in a game reserve watching a giraffe nibble tree leaves. "I know Americans when I see them!" he bellowed, grinning, vigorously shaking my hand. "The minute I saw y'all, I said to my wife, 'I bet you they're Americans!' " Southern drawls had always raised the hair on my neck and arms, but his was as comforting as a favorite song. I wanted nothing more, at that moment, than to board the nearest US-bound plane.

For six weeks, while Brenda studied in the national archives, we learned the rules of this new race game, and we played it as best we could. But those were city rules. The rules in the Matebeland countryside were different. To many of the people living in thatched, clay homes, whose annual income was less than five dollars, we were *amakiwa,* white people, people whose likely purpose for being there was to make their fortunes rise or fall. This knowledge made me uneasy, because I knew, on some level, their kindness was based on fear or desire. And it also made me thankful, because whatever it was we inspired, it got us what we wanted. No one refused an interview. We took pictures at will.

One day while we were taking pictures, a young boy sprinted over to us and began speaking hurriedly in isiNdebele to our translator. After he finished, our translator said, "We are wanted by the headman. Over there." He pointed toward a gazebo-like structure a hundred yards away. We could not see anyone from our distance, but when we arrived, we found four men inside, sitting on straw mats and playing mancala, a popular game made of carved wood and plant seeds. The men continued to play with intense purpose, as if something so costly were at stake they could not pause to acknowledge our arrival. Our translator sat along the base of the wall and watched quietly. Brenda and I followed his lead.

One of the men made a move that ended the game. As the good-natured banter that followed tapered off, the man who had won said something to our translator. When the response included the word *Americans,* the man's eyes sparkled. "Welcome!" he said, speaking to me but not Brenda, as rural men often did. "I am Msizi Nkosi, the headman of this village." I had not expected him to speak English. He seemed proud of this fact, and after his greeting, and after every question he subsequently asked, he offered his comrades a quick wink.

Most of what he wanted to know was aimed at confirming or dispelling rumors about American culture, things about gangsters, Madonna, and sports. "This Michael Jordan is better than all the others," he said. "You see, he is like me playing mancala with these men here." He laughed heartily before his face settled on the wry smile that never left it, even when his questions took a twisted turn. "Tell me, my friend. Are you happy that your ancestors were taken to be slaves to America?"

"*Of course* not," I said.

"Ah, but I wish *my* ancestors were made slaves there," he said. "Because then I would be living the good life, like you."

I had heard variations on this reasoning before, the notion that blacks should view their history through the lens of capitalism, a lens that often values means less than ends, humanity less than goods. What about the brutality the slaves endured? The suffering? The rapes and murders? I tried to make this point, but the headman was having none of it. "Ah, but you must not dwell on these things," he countered. "You are in America, so just be happy. Or would you rather be here, losing games of mancala to me?" I did not respond. He winked at the other men. I looked toward our translator, lifting and lowering my eyebrows, trying to communicate nonverbally that we should go. When I caught his attention, he nodded, but I wasn't sure if it was to say *Yes, let's get away from this crazy person,* or *Yes, you are in America, so just be happy.*

"Tell me," the headman continued. "Why do you people call yourselves *African* Americans?"

I considered explaining that it was a way to offer a sense of belonging to a displaced people, but my heart wasn't in the argument, so I said nothing.

"You are *not* Africans," he said. His smile remained, but his voice had a sharp edge to it now. "Do you know that you *insult* Africans when you say that you are one of us?" I still did not respond.

But I did wonder, during our ride back into town, what the headman's definition of an African was. I wondered how he viewed his white countrymen, people whose ancestors had arrived from England two centuries prior and had taken over the land. Maybe he didn't see them as Africans either. Or maybe they were the *only* Africans, while the blacks were something else, *something more*—perhaps that was what was being conveyed by the phrase *indigenous peoples* that Brenda and I had heard frequently since our arrival. I wondered, too, what the headman would have thought of Farai, a black native who had made a fortune in banking, now owned a taxi service and rental properties, and lived in a house that could have passed for a small Marriott. What would the headman have thought of her Olympic-sized pool, her tennis court, the crystal chandeliers and marble floors and ceilings made of inlaid cedar? What would he have thought watching her field servants toil all day in rows of maize and potatoes, or watching her house servants cooking, cleaning, babysitting, and laundering until they collapsed in the shacks behind the house that had neither electricity nor running water?

And what, I wondered, would the headman have thought of "African night"?

"*What* night?" Brenda had said at its first mention. We had been in the country for about ten days then.

"African night," Farai said. "I have invited some of my friends to join us for a girls' night out, and we have decided to call it *African* night." This, she explained while giggling, would entail wearing traditional African clothes. Farai did not own any of these clothes, nor did any of her friends; they had to go to the mall to purchase them explicitly for this occasion. It was the same mall to which they'd return for dinner, where there was a restaurant popular among tourists because it served mopane, a local delicacy of deep-fried caterpillars. When the plates of mopane arrived, the women shrieked and gasped and refused to eat them. And then they went back to their vodka martinis while the cook prepared their new orders of apricot-glazed chicken with peaches and raisins.

I'd thought of my sister Linda, and all the other people I knew who regularly wore African garments, and here were these genuine Africans, these indigenous peoples, wearing the clothing as if for Halloween or a masquerade. Brenda and I had found the irony of all this hilarious. When she'd returned from the restaurant, her head and body still adorned in yards of colorful patterned cotton, we'd stayed up late into the night laughing until our eyes watered, because so many things were still funny then. But not much was funny anymore. Just confusing. The only thing that was clear was that, whatever the definition of an African was, it did not apply to me. Neither did the words *colored* or *amakiwa*. I was black, plain and simple, and in the days leading up to our departure I looked forward to reclaiming this identity because, before I actually boarded the plane, I still thought I could.

But the truth hit me during the flight, bringing with it that sickening feeling I sometimes get while driving to a new destination when I suddenly realize that I am lost. Occasionally the source of the error can be traced to someone's faulty directions, though usually the mistake is mine for not paying attention. I prefer when it's the former so I can dole out rather than accept the blame. Now, cruising at thirty-thousand feet, I considered the directions I had been given regarding race, which made no mention of how unfixed it is, how fluid, how utterly *unscientific* the process by which we assign and accept racial labels. *Who,* I wondered, could I blame for this?

When I reached a few tentative conclusions, I shook Brenda's shoulder, waking her. She turned to face me, wide-eyed, I could see from the dim light of the cabin, and asked me what was wrong.

"My parents," I said, "messed me up."

After a brief pause, just long enough for the pupils of her widened eyes to roll, she mumbled, "How *this* time?"

"I'm not *entirely* sure."

"Well, when you are entirely sure, let me know." She turned away, burrowing her head back into the pillow she'd propped between her shoulder and the window.

"*You* messed me up, too," I added, but I'd whispered it so she could not hear, since I wasn't entirely sure how she had done so either. But I suspected it was related to a story she'd once told me about a boy named Billy. When she met him, she was six years old and attending a mostly white school. Besides her, Billy was the only other black student. When some of the other children refused to play with him because of his race, Brenda refused, too, banding with the white kids who had accepted her as one of their own. That night at dinner, she told her parents, "We didn't play with Billy today because he's black," thereby triggering an enlightening discussion about race in general, her African father in particular, and her own 50 percent blackness.

I remembered this story making me sad—not for Brenda; she was fine, even playing with Billy the next day and persuading her friends to do the same—but because my parents had never had such a discussion with my siblings and me. There was never a moment when they told us we were black, or that they were, or what that designation meant for any of us. Race, in fact, was rarely discussed in the household of my youth. It was only while in the company of friends and relatives that I overheard grown-ups pontificate on racial matters, often concluding their observations with a shake of the head and the phrase, "Black folks are *something else*."

When I was very young, I thought this was an unkind reference to the prostitutes and addicts who shared our housing project stairwell, but by the time I turned ten, in 1974, when a new positive racial awareness was at its height, I understood it to mean that blacks were beautiful. Blacks were cool. Blacks had style and nerve and they could dance, dribble balls, and sing. Being black also now meant being African, a descendant of kings and queens, and while we did not learn that from our parents either, many people we knew spoke of it in the same breath they said that whites were evil. A few altercations I would have with white teens would reinforce this latter view; a few altercations I would have with white police would confirm it.

But my exposure over time to a wider variety of people chipped away at all of these stereotypes; not many remained, I felt, by the time I turned twenty-five. By age thirty I was convinced they were completely gone, only to have them surface, one year later, in a country not my own, like a suddenly remembered dream. As soon as Brenda and I were told we were colored, I realized how many negative beliefs I had internalized about white people, beliefs that were still very much with me, whether consciously or not. But if my race could change so easily without any fundamental change in me, then race had no meaning, other than the false or superficial ones assigned it. All human behavior associated with race was a myth, a lie. I have found nothing in life more unsettling, or more liberating, than that discovery.

Except for maybe this: I now understood that my parents knew all along what they were doing by not engaging us in discussions about race. They were trying to teach us, through their silence, that race was insignificant, that it shouldn't and ultimately didn't matter. They were trying to teach us to see character, not skin. These, I realized on that long flight home, were my parents' directions for how to be an American. And I had not paid attention.

FLOATED

*B*uggy was a Vietnam vet who sometimes used liquor instead of pot. He'd be standing in his usual place in front of his parents' house, his back grazing a high hedge as he took swigs from a bottle of rum. When he finished drinking he would laugh, curse, cry, throw punches, or stare blankly at a tree. But because this was what he always did, we assumed liquor had no special effect on him, or that, being crazy, nothing affected him at all.

"He can't feel liquor," Zack said one night when the topic was raised. We were drinking liquor ourselves—peppermint schnapps—and it had affected us very much. The bottle was almost empty, an entire pint consumed in less than an hour in my garage. "Once you're crazy," Zack said, elaborating on his point, "you're protected against any and all further mind alteration."

Greg agreed. "Like being dead."

"Exactly," Zack responded.

A car passed slowly in the alley, its wheels crunching the gravel. We froze, fearing the police, and then moved closer to the door. Louis opened it a crack and we all peeked out. A white Oldsmobile crept away, its high beams scattering a cluster of rats. After the door was closed we drifted back toward the center of the room. Above us, gnats attacked a lightbulb. Zack continued talking about Buggy. "I saw him drink a whole quart of rum once, and it didn't faze him."

"Bull*shit,*" Greg said.

"No lie," Zack insisted. "He didn't even fall."

"He fell," Louis chimed in.

Zack looked at Louis. "No, he didn't."

"He *did.*"

"How you going to tell me what I saw, nigger? I was *there.*"

"And *I* was with you," Louis countered. "We were standing in front of my house watching him when he fell backward into the hedges. You even said, 'Damn, Buggy's so drunk he fell in the hedges.' "

Zack clarified his position. "I wasn't speaking *technically*," he said. "*Technically,* he didn't fall because he never hit the ground. You have to hit the ground to fall. It was more like, you know, he floated."

We all stared at Zack for a few seconds. Greg cleared his throat. When he spoke, his voice was almost a whisper. "Zack," he asked, "are you retarded?"

Zack slapped him. Greg returned a blow. Then razors were drawn and they were yelling, "I'll kill you!" Louis and I backed away while they circled each other, their weapons raised, missiles ready for launch. Zack was the more violent of the two and had studied Tae Kwon Do, but peppermint schnapps had leveled the field. A kick to the gut sent him staggering backward and tumbling over a folding chair. He landed on a pile of plywood stacked near the wall. Before he stood he cupped his right cheek and then checked his hand for blood. There wasn't any. Unconvinced, he checked it again. "You all right?" I asked. Zack didn't respond. He rubbed his wound, lightly moving his fingers over a small area that seemed to swell beneath his touch. He checked for blood once more before he stood and brushed himself off. He still had his razor in his hand. Greg still had his. I offered Zack the bottle.

He hesitated before accepting it. He took a deep swallow and gave it back to me. I handed it to Greg, who took a turn and handed it to Louis. No one spoke until the cycle was repeated and the liquor was gone. Zack motioned his razor toward the plywood. "Technically," he said, "I floated, too."

SIMPLICITY

*I*n 1992 I'd proposed to Brenda with a ring purchased with a student loan. We toyed with the idea of having a wedding with all the bells and whistles, but racking up thousands of dollars of debt in the process wasn't an option, because that rack was already full. Besides, we felt there was great romance in simplicity. And so on May 11, 1995, with a justice of the peace and with two friends as witnesses, we stood in our backyard and took our vows in front of a garden of blooming tulips. For the occasion, I'd bought a new suit with money borrowed from my parents. Brenda wore the gown we'd purchased four years earlier at Neiman Marcus.

Later that spring, our trip to Zimbabwe had served as a honeymoon, as we would not have been able to afford one otherwise. In 1996 we returned to Zimbabwe to conduct more research, and this time we stayed for nearly a year, three weeks of which were spent touring South Africa on, unofficially, honeymoon number two. But once we returned to Iowa City in the summer of 1997, we settled back into the lives of the have-nots, barely scraping by on the university's money. Brenda received a small stipend to write her dissertation and serve as a teaching assistant, and I received an even smaller stipend for taking classes toward a doctoral degree that I had no intention of earning, since I had no desire to teach.

My only desire was to defer repaying my student loans indefinitely, and to avoid gainful employment even longer. So I'd decided to continue studying black literature and culture with James Alan McPherson until Brenda graduated and became a wealthy college professor. Meanwhile, we'd continue to live on generic-brand foods. We'd continue to shop at Goodwill. In winter we'd continue to wear layers of clothing inside our house and scrape ice off our windows to look outside. And we would continue struggling to pay our mortgage, which would continue to upset my mother-in-law because she had purchased the small four-room ranch where Brenda and I lived. The easy solution to our financial strain, my mother-in-law often said, was for me to get a job.

"Writing is my job," I'd respond.

"No, a real one."

"It is a real one."

"A real job pays," she'd say.

"Maybe someday my writing will."

"Or maybe someday houses will be free."

My family was no better. They simply could not comprehend how I'd left the medical center in order to attend college and graduate school, only to end up as poor as a brother still in the hood. "All you're missing is food stamps," my father said to me once, "and a bunch of babies." We did not qualify for food stamps—I'd checked—nor, it seemed, for a bunch of babies. Soon after our second trip to Zimbabwe, we'd begun attempting to start a family, assuming that our mere desire for children would have them tumble forth, like so many spilled beans. A year later we were still trying. "Maybe," my father said, "God is trying to tell you something."

"What?"

"To get a job," he said. "Or to finish your PhD."

"I don't want either."

"But you might need both," he responded, and then, as was

the case more and more, his thoughts drifted into the past, this time coming to rest in the year he and my mother were married.

That was 1955. My mother had just graduated from high school and my father had just dropped out. He'd only been a year from finishing, but he wanted to support his new bride and to not have to live with his grandmother for more than a few weeks. He began working full-time as a Braille instructor. His position paid minimum wage, which would allow him and my mother no luxuries, save for the most important one—the ability to live independent lives. This, for my parents, as it no doubt is for most people with disabilities, was a big deal. It was with a tremendous sense of accomplishment, then, that my father moved my mother to their very own two-room apartment in the projects. And it was with a tremendous sense of failure, three months later, when my mother announced she was expecting a child, that my father realized he hadn't thought his life through.

The only thing he'd given much thought to since meeting my mother was their happiness. He hadn't factored in children or given any consideration to what would make them happy too, but he knew that living in the projects wasn't it. Even in the 1950s the ABLA Homes was an unsafe place; being blind, he couldn't watch over and protect his children, and so there was no way he'd let them go outside to play. They would need a house with a fenced backyard, and he vowed, the moment my mother placed his hand on her stomach, to buy them one. In time I would fully appreciate the sacrifices he had been willing to make, but as I tried unsuccessfully to start my own family, I could not do so. That's why a job, a real one that paid, was not high on my list of priorities, and neither was completing a doctorate. Maybe that was why it was so difficult for us to conceive; maybe God *was* trying to tell me something, namely that my life, like my newly married father's, had not been thought through.

This message must have been getting across, because my father was on my mind a lot in those days, the uncanny symmetry of our lives. After dropping out of high school, we both decided to return, me in 1982 for my GED, my father in 1957 to complete his final year. We both attended community colleges. We both transferred to four-year universities. I'd earned a bachelor's and a master's degree, and he had too. I had no interest in earning a PhD, but, thinking about my father, I now knew that I would. My father had been interested in earning a PhD, but, thinking about his children, he now knew that he couldn't. He needed to find a job.

He worked first as a counselor of children with disabilities, and then he became a teacher. From the time he'd first placed his hand on my mother's stomach to the time he taught his first class, most of the clothes he'd worn had been donated by his church, the food he'd eaten rarely varied from grits and beans, the welfare checks and food stamps he received had torn at his pride, and the strain of poverty had jeopardized his marriage. At last, fourteen years after he vowed to buy a house, he led his wife, and their now six children, through the front door. I could only imagine the pride and joy he felt at that moment. And I'd hoped that, one day, our lives would have that symmetry too.

THE SECOND ACT

We hadn't intended to rob her but the opportunity was there—an elderly woman carrying a grocery bag into her house while two more bags sat in the opened trunk of her car. Steve grabbed one and I grabbed the other. We sprinted for a block and then jogged the rest of the way to my house to assess our booty: eight cans of tomato soup, two loaves of bread, twenty-four ounces of orange-flavored Metamucil, eight pounds of chicken fryers, lard, a bag of chips, and a pair of Dr. Scholl's inserts. I opened the chips. Steve put the inserts in his shoes. The elderly lady, I assumed, called the police.

Or maybe she called God. I imagined her standing by her empty trunk with her hands raised toward the sky, asking that the robbers be brought to justice. But I knew the justice she sought already awaited me. I had heard my parents and various ministers repeatedly speak of the lake of fire, and yet such talk had not deterred me from seeking my place there. Eternal damnation, the way I saw it, would simply be the second act, a continuation of the life I already led, day after day filled with debauchery and nights with more of the same. The lake of fire did not concern me. So I wasn't sure what it was that made me say we should return the groceries.

Steve was appalled. "You want to do what?"

"Return the groceries," I repeated. "Let's take them back."

A smirk spread on his face. "What's wrong with you, feeling bad for the little old lady?"

I ignored him.

"Maybe you'd like to take her some flowers, too." He was using a whiny voice now, mimicking a bratty child. "Here, little old lady, I brought you your chicken and some roses . . ."

I took my razor out of my sock and pointed it at his neck. His smirk faded. "Don't play with that thing," he said, a statement of formality because he knew I wasn't playing. I had a big problem with being teased and everybody knew it. And I'd been drinking. I backed him toward the door. As soon as he stepped outside he ran, and I ran after him, the razor still in my hand, even though it was midday and someone could have seen me. But the streets were deserted, as were the backyards and alleys we zigzagged through before I let him go. I tucked the razor back into my sock and went home to get the groceries.

The old lady's street was as empty as mine had been. Her car was still parked in front of her house, only the trunk was closed now. So was her front door. The windows that flanked it were opened a few inches and guarded by burglar bars. I climbed the stairs to her porch planning to ring the bell and flee, leaving the groceries for her discovery. But as I was about to set them down, the door opened. The old lady stood before me now, looking confused.

"I . . . I saw someone take these from your car," I mumbled. "Some kid, a stupid teenager. I chased him and got them back for you."

She joined me on the porch. I held out the bags for her. As she took them, our hands briefly touched. "God bless you," she said.

But I didn't hear her, not for many years.

SCATTERED INCONVENIENCES

*H*e barreled up on our left, momentarily matched our speed, then surged forward and waved a cowboy hat out the window, a bull rider in a brown Chevy. Somehow I knew he would swerve into our lane and slow down, and as he did the sound of his horn came to us over the rumble of our truck's engine. We were in a seventeen-foot Ryder that held everything we owned, junk, pretty much, with ten feet to spare. Those were, we believed, the final days of poverty. After not being able to find a teaching position for three years since completing her doctorate, Brenda had landed a rare tenure-track position at a state college in New England, twelve hundred miles east of Iowa City where we'd spent ten years living with tornadoes, academics, and hippies. I was going to be a stay-at-home dad, watching our fifteen-month-old during the day and writing at night. It was the perfect scenario, one we'd dreamed of for so long. All I had to do now was prevent the man in the Chevy from killing us.

I gripped the steering wheel tighter, checked the rearview mirrors in case a sudden maneuver was necessary. There were no vehicles within twenty yards, besides our reckless escort, just ten feet away.

"This guy's drunk or something," Brenda said.

I shook my head. "I *told you* we shouldn't drive in the middle of the night."

"It's only eight," Brenda responded.

I checked the clock on the dashboard. "Eight ten."

"Well, you could just *slow down*," she said, "and let him go."

"Or," I responded, "I could crush him."

"And injure your son in the process?"

I glanced to my right. Adrian slept between us in his child seat, oblivious that we were being menaced by a fool and that his daddy, in certain situations, particularly those that involved motor vehicles and testosterone, was a fool, too. I tugged at his harness, confirmed that it was secure, then gunned the engine and lurched the truck forward. Brenda punched my arm. I lifted my foot off the accelerator and watched the speedometer topple from seventy to fifty-five, where I leveled off. For a few seconds there was a gentlemanly distance between us and the Chevy, and then it slowed, too, until it was again ten feet from our bumper. This time I held my ground. I could feel Brenda tensing. The man waved his hat some more. I lowered my window and gave him the finger, Adrian stirring as wind tore into the cab. Brenda called me a jerk, though not audibly. We'd been together long enough that the actual use of words, at times like those, was unnecessary.

The Chevy suddenly braked and I had to as well to avoid a collision. My heart was racing now. I tried hard to believe that we weren't dealing with something more ominous than a souse. We were in Indiana, a state I vaguely remembered hearing was a breeding ground for racists; perhaps the random sight of a black family had proved too irresistible, a cat straying into an angry dog's view.

But I had heard similar things about Iowa, only to experience no problems. *No problems* is not to say *nothing*, though, for there were what a black intellectual referred to as "scattered inconveniences"—

women crossing the street or removing their purses from grocery carts at my approach, security guards following me in department stores. Once, while I was working out in the university's gym, two young men, looking my way and laughing, began mimicking the walk of a gorilla. Silly, all of it, confirmation that the bigotry my parents faced no longer exists, that its sledgehammer impact has been reduced, for the most part, to pebbles pitched from a naughty child's hand. I tell myself to find victory in encounters such as these. And I usually do. But sometimes I can't because of one simple truth: I am a racist.

Like a recovering alcoholic, I recognize that to define myself by my disease is in some way to help guard against relapse, that there is daily salvation in this constant reminder of who and what I am. My quest to be rid of all traces of this scourge has not been easy, though I have made good progress, considering some of the things I'd heard about whites since the time I was a child. Whites discriminated against us. Whites denied us decent housing. Whites caused us to have high unemployment and failed schools. Crack had come from whites, and so had AIDS. Whites, in some vague and yet indisputable way, made the winos drink and gang-bangers kill. I came to believe, at a very early age, that in order to succeed I would have to beat the system through the mastery of some criminal enterprise, or join it in the form of a Sambo, a sell-out, an Oreo. In other words, I'd have to be my brother Tommy.

Tommy, who said things like "Whites aren't an obstacle to success," and "Only *you* can stop *you*."

We didn't like Tommy.

We watched him with disgust as he became a teenager and continued to speak without slang or profanity. He wore straight-legs and loafers instead of bell-bottoms and four-inch stacks, his only concession to soulful style an Afro, which *could* have been bigger. He held a job during high school and still earned straight

A's. After graduation he studied computers when his friends aspired to be postal clerks or pimps.

After our father threw him out for fighting with Jimmy, it was many years before I saw him socially again, other than at church. I didn't know where he spent his exile. I was not surprised, though, when he resurfaced in the 1980s in a Ford Aerostar with a Ronald Reagan sticker on his bumper. He'd rejected victim ideology his whole life, and so his emergence as a staunch conservative made perfect sense, as much sense as me, twenty years later, being tempted to crush a white man on I-80.

The Chevy switched lanes again, this time to the right. The driver was shouting at us through his opened window. I ignored him. He blew his horn.

Brenda asked, "What do you think he wants?"

"Our lives," I said.

He blew his horn again.

"I'm going to open my window," Brenda replied, "and see what he wants."

"Do *not* do that!"

She opened her window. I couldn't make out what he was saying, and Brenda was practically hanging out the window to hear him. I leaned toward them while trying to keep the truck steady. Brenda suddenly whirled to face me. Her eyes were filled with terror. "Stop the truck!" she demanded.

"*Why?*"

"The back door is open! The washer's about to fall out!"

We were towing our car behind us; the perilousness of the situation was instantly clear.

I put on my right signal and began to work my way to the shoulder. The man tooted his horn and gave me a thumbs-up, then rode off into the night. Adrian was crying and I wondered for how long. His pacifier had fallen. Brenda rooted it from his seat and slipped it between his lips. He puffed on it fiendishly, like it was long-denied nicotine.

We'd come to a stop. Our hazards were flashing. Cars and trucks rocked us gently as they hurled themselves east, toward the Promised Land. Before I opened my door, Brenda and I exchanged a quick glance. I did not have to actually say I was sorry. She did not have to actually say she forgave me.

MY SISTER'S ROOMMATE

Somewhere near Oak Lawn, Tim began steering with his knee. Every once in a while a gust of wind would push against the car, causing it to veer left or right and his girlfriend to scream. Tim would tell her to relax as he grabbed the wheel, and I'd take another swallow of whiskey. Other than that we crept steadily along through the snow, our car the only one on the highway, our wipers making the only sound. I wished the radio worked. I wished I hadn't come.

I tapped Tim's shoulder and handed him the bottle. He took a drink, chased it with his beer, and then reached above the visor to remove a small piece of paper. After turning on the cabin light, he passed the paper to Karen. I sat forward and watched as she unfolded the sides until the powder was visible. She scooped some up on a long, chipped nail and raised it to a nostril. She fed the other one before passing the coke to me. I'd never tried it before so I looked to Tim for reassurance; he nodded that it was okay. I took a hit and instantly knew invincibility. A two-hour road trip through a snowstorm, it was clear to me now, was a very reasonable idea.

"So," Tim began, making eye contact with me in the rearview mirror. "You excited to meet Linda's new roommate?"

I didn't answer because I knew where this was headed.

"You'll like her," he continued. "And she'll like you. I told her about you the last time I was there. She was extremely eager to meet you. So, little bro', looks like this will be your lucky night, unless you're a sissy." He faced Karen and added, "Jerry just turned sixteen and he *still* hasn't had any pussy." They both laughed and I hated Tim right then. But after another hit of coke, his teasing seemed reasonable too.

At around 4:00 AM we were in Charleston, Illinois, where Linda was attending college, swaying on the porch of a duplex that Tim believed to be where she lived. Karen was leaning heavily against him, either to remain upright or to guard against the brutal winds, and I stood on his other side. I rang the bell. When no one responded, Tim rapped the door with his beer bottle. A moment later, in the window to our left, fingertips parted the blinds.

Linda opened the door in sweats. After noting the hour and our recklessness, she let us in and insisted we go to bed. She went upstairs and returned with blankets and pillows. She would sleep on the recliner in the study, she said, while I would get the couch; Tim and Karen would take her room. Linda and I watched them stumble up the stairs before she let me have it. "Don't you have any more sense," she scolded me, "than to drive around with your drunk brother in the middle of the night? What were you thinking?"

At that moment I was thinking I wanted to sleep. So I remained quiet, even as the tone of her lecture softened and she urged me to get myself together. I sat on the couch, fixed my face with a look of deep remorse, and drifted off to the sound of her voice.

Another voice woke me. "You don't have to sleep on the couch," it whispered. It was too dark to see, and for a second I thought I was dreaming. "Come upstairs in ten minutes," the voice said again, and I knew it had to be my sister's roommate. "It's the room on the right," she continued, a little closer to me now, her breath warm on my ear. My heart raced as I listened to the squeak of the hardwood floor, the fading shuffle of slippers.

Ten minutes is a long time when you're about to lose your virginity. What do you do, except think stupid thoughts? Like how maybe I didn't really want to go upstairs. Maybe I was only considering it because Tim had teased me. Maybe I was a sissy. Ten minutes is a short time when you're trying to figure out who you are.

I went to the bathroom, splashed cold water on my face, and looked in the mirror. The person looking back had bloodshot eyes, disheveled hair, and bushy eyebrows sticking up in places. He seemed like he might be wasted. But what did any of that tell me? I leaned closer to him. "Who are you?" I asked. *"Who are you?"* He didn't answer. I went upstairs.

A yellow streetlight outside the window cast the room in an eerie hue. After my eyes adjusted, I looked around but there wasn't much to see: a desk, dresser, stereo, two lamps, and a pile of clothes heaped in a corner. A bed was against the far wall, and on it my sister's roommate lay with her back toward me, covered in a puffy black quilt. I thought to say her name but I didn't know it, so I walked to the side of her bed. "I'm here," I said. She didn't reply. "I'm here," I said again, a little louder this time. "You told me to come up in ten minutes." She still didn't answer. I was about to leave when she rolled onto her back and raised the quilt off her nude body, like a vampire lifting its cape.

She was huge. Easily over three hundred pounds. Her face was swollen with fat, making her eyes two little raisins, sunken in a mound of fudge. Crusts of something white lined her upper lip. I hesitated, but I didn't have the nerve to leave. I sat on the side of the bed and removed my shirt. I slid my pants and underwear down my legs and onto the floor before lying next to her. The sheets smelled of sweat; her body was faintly sticky.

"Promise me you won't tell anyone," she whispered.

I promised.

COMMUNION

We'd searched the Web and this was what we knew: Bridgewater, Massachusetts, incorporated in 1656; twenty-five miles south of Boston; population, 25,185. Only 4 percent of these residents were black, which was significantly below the national average. But we weren't looking for blacks per se. We were looking for open-mindedness. That's what we'd found in Iowa City, a college town with similar demographics, and what we were hoping for in the college town we'd be moving to.

However, Brenda's interview for a teaching position at Bridgewater State College revealed that this was not a college town, but rather a town with a college, and that the relationship between the two was uneasy. Sixty-five percent of the students were commuters, intellectual transients in a land of incomes earned largely through service and manual labor. There were no quaint bakeries. There was a tattoo parlor and a bikers' café. There were no Starbucks or expansive used-book stores. There was a state prison. "If you do get the position," Brenda was warned by a member of the faculty during her interview, "*do not* move to Bridgewater." And then, when she got the position, she received urgent phone calls from the same person reminding her not to settle there. "Trust me," her new colleague said. "It's *crawling* with rednecks and bigots."

Brenda had found this hard to believe. I, however, felt we were in no position to dispute these claims. I called a real estate company based south of Boston and scheduled a visit to see area listings. *"Excluding,"* I stressed, "Bridgewater."

"Didn't you say your wife will be teaching at Bridgewater State College?" the agent asked.

"Yes."

"And yet you don't want to live in Bridgewater?"

"Under no circumstances."

"Any particular reason?"

"None that I am prepared to say."

"But it's *such* a beautiful city."

Bull Connor, I thought to myself, *must have said the same of Birmingham.*

Our visit took place in June. It went poorly, for the most part because we were poor. After a week of house hunting, we flew back to Iowa City, stunned by New England housing prices and convinced we'd never qualify for a mortgage. Our house in Iowa had cost forty-six thousand dollars. There was nothing suitable south of Boston and outside of Bridgewater for under a quarter million.

We went back on the Web, this time to search for rentals. They were overpriced, too. We ended up choosing a vast apartment complex located three blocks from the college in a gated community. A two-bedroom unit was twelve hundred a month, a ridiculous sum that was about four times the size of our mortgage payment. I felt pretty good about the gate, though.

We arrived at dusk. An elderly man in the gatehouse watched us approach. He did not return my smile when I pulled the truck up to his side window. In fact, he looked angry. A closed-circuit monitor sat on his desk flashing images from around this small, exclusive city. Next to the monitor was a television; a baseball game was

on. I gestured toward it and asked, "Who's winning?" He faced
me but gave no reply. I looked at Brenda; she shrugged. I looked
back at the elderly man. He was concentrating on the game now,
as if our business there was done.

The pitcher threw a curveball that caught the outside corner.
The next pitch was high and inside. I cleared my throat. "We're
moving in," I said. "There are supposed to be keys here for me,
Jerald Walker." The batter popped out and the elderly man swore.
He opened a file cabinet and thumbed through a stack of manila
folders, pulling one from the back and handing it to me. After racing through an incomprehensible set of directions and something
about the rental office and our lease, he pressed a red button on
the wall. The gate in front of us rose. I heard the old man swear
again as I put the truck in gear. I concentrated, then, on the scene
before us.

"This is *so* nice," Brenda said.

And it was. Lush and immaculately maintained lawns. Flower
beds. A swimming pool, tennis and basketball courts. Children
riding bicycles. There were a couple of joggers and people seemingly out for an evening stroll. A NATURE TRAIL sign pointed
toward sprawling woods a few hundred yards away. We rounded a
tight corner just as a young woman emerged from building sixty-
eight. She noticed us rolling by and waved. Brenda and I returned
the gesture, but Adrian, wisely holding his cards close to the vest,
stared at her blankly. And then I saw it: a minivan cruising toward
us with a black family inside. My hands relaxed on the steering
wheel. "Thank *God,*" I said, "we're not the only Negroes here."

We lapped the complex twice, then at last found our building
and disembarked. When we entered the hall, I noticed that the
maroon carpet looked new and the air carried a pleasant hint of
lemon. Our unit was on the ground floor, conveniently located
across from the laundry room. I unlocked our door and led us inside.

All but one of the windows faced north. We basically would receive no direct sun, which was fine for now, but I knew its midwinter absence would sink me into a full-scale depression. The kitchen had no windows at all, so it wasn't until we turned on the light that we saw the roaches. The bathroom's exhaust vent was a tunnel to a cigarette smoker. The walls were thin, the carpet was mysteriously crunchy, and the ceiling was low enough that a man of average height, say, me, for instance, could reach up and poke a water spot with his finger. This was what I was doing when Brenda said, "I'm not staying here."

I lowered my arm. "We don't have a choice."

"We have to buy a house. You have to get a teaching position."

"I don't want a teaching position."

She put Adrian down. He staggered a few steps and then lowered himself to crawl. "As soon as we get settled, I'll stop by the English office and introduce myself to the chair."

"But even if," I said, trying a different approach, "even if I *could* land a teaching position, we still won't be able to afford a house."

"In Bridgewater we can."

I did a double take. *"With the rednecks and bigots?"*

"Well, we're not staying *here*."

I put my arm around her shoulders. "I'm afraid we are."

A few weeks later I was in the faculty dining room having lunch with the English Department chair, a blind date arranged by Brenda. They might have a position soon, the chair told me, for someone to teach African American literature and creative writing. She straddled her salad with her elbows and interlocked her fingers beneath her chin. Her manicure reflected the overhead lights. "And what are you completing your doctorate in?"

"African American literature," I said, "and creative writing."

"How *perfect!*"

I explained that I was not in the market for a job, that I was a stay-at-home dad, enjoying my days with my son and evenings with my work. "I'm a writer," I said.

She winked. "Aren't we all?"

The rednecks and bigots were very coy. After six weeks we had been neither insulted nor injured. At worst, the locals had greeted us with indifference, which, someone explained, was simply the New England way. That was taking some getting used to, as well as the way they talked. We were considering homeschooling Adrian.

"It's not the accent you have to worry about," a colleague of Brenda's told us over lunch. "It's the racists." She was the person who had repeatedly warned us not to move there.

"So far everyone's been really nice," Brenda said.

The colleague snickered. "They're just feeling you out. Give them time. Just don't lower your guard."

I assured her that on no occasion would I let that happen. She smiled at me and took a sip of her Singha. We were in a Thai restaurant, one of the few places to dine in Bridgewater that served international cuisine. It was our favorite local place to eat, and it was also a favorite of the college. Usually half of the thirty or so tables were occupied by faculty, students, and staff, pretty much the way certain businesses in Iowa City were occupied by the University of Iowa's family. Each time we went there, I was reminded of what we had left behind: international food; friends; a sense of community; racial tolerance; affordable housing; the Queen's English. More and more our decision to leave felt wrong.

Late October. The twin towers were gone, three thousand were dead, and Brenda was pregnant. In our grief, we'd decided to have another baby, procreation as therapy. Communion as therapy, too; we felt a desperate need to feel a part of our new town. And so there we were, a few days before Halloween, on an unseasonably warm afternoon, standing in front of the house in Bridgewater we hoped to buy.

It was a four-bedroom Greek Revival, built in 1920. The listing price was one hundred thousand less than any decent-looking property we'd seen in the region. And it was only half a block from the campus, which was a definite plus, since we owned just one car. Brenda and I had spent the night crunching numbers. With her grandmother's assistance for the down payment, we thought we could make ends meet without me needing to teach. We'd have to make a number of sacrifices, all of which would be worth it to have a yard, to not listen to our neighbors beat on the walls when Adrian cried, and to shake the cabin fever that already had me in its hold.

A silver SUV rocked across the crumbling driveway. It parked behind our car. A moment later a robust, middle-aged woman emerged and waved. "I'm Ingrid," she said. "And you must be Jerald." I shook her hand before introducing Brenda and Adrian. Then there was an awkward silence during which we all faced the house, as if it would speak. "Well, well, well," Ingrid said. She moved toward the stairs leading to the back door. We followed her.

There was a lockbox on the handle, which Ingrid battled for a moment before at last removing the key and thrusting it upward. "Success!" she said. We entered and began the tour.

I beelined for the picture window. "This is east, isn't it?"

Ingrid thought for a moment. "Yes."

I imagined lying right there on the floor, the morning sun irradiating my winter blues like cancer cells. I'd seen all I needed to see. Brenda hadn't, though, and she combed every inch of the house, concluding her survey on the second floor, deep in the master closet, its door squeaking closed behind her. She popped out a second later, beaming, a hopeless fish on Ingrid's line. "There's a lot of space in there!" she announced.

Ingrid smiled sweetly. "So, would you like to make an offer?"

Just then a loud horn startled us. We drifted toward a window and watched a locomotive chug our way, where in seconds it passed not far on our right, sounding its deafening blast. Ingrid cupped Adrian's ears. Brenda and I cupped ours. The house seemed to shake and rumble. Somewhere nearby, I imagined, a Richter scale flashed a two.

"That was *fun!*" Adrian squealed. "Do it again, do it again!"

Ingrid smiled and pinched his cheek. "Not for another thirty minutes, sweetie."

Brenda looked at me and asked, "That wasn't so bad, was it?"

I shook my head. "No, not at all."

We agreed to meet Ingrid at her office to do the paperwork.

Outside, as we approached our cars, we saw a man standing in the backyard near a splintered oak tree. A bad feeling suddenly descended on me. "Who's that?" I asked.

"I don't know," Ingrid responded.

The man moved toward the house. Ingrid said hello. He smiled and waved at us as he mounted the stairs. He removed a key from his pocket and let himself inside.

Ingrid said, "Must be the owner."

"Must be," Brenda agreed.

At Ingrid's office, respecting our desperation and the fast seller's market, we offered full price. Ingrid was friends with the listing Realtor and promised to call him right away. She congratulated and hugged us before we left.

We decided to celebrate. We stopped at an ice cream stand for three scoops of Oreo Crunch. Adrian had baptized himself in his by the time we reached the apartment, but we were too happy to care. Laughing, we took him inside to give him a bath. Brenda started filling the tub, but after looking beneath the vanity saw that there was no Mr. Bubble. I headed to the kitchen cupboard in search of more.

When I turned on the light, a few tiny roaches ran for cover. One dodged behind the phone, I noticed, as I reached for the receiver to check for messages. There were two. The first one was from my mother, who wanted to know if we'd put an offer on the house, and the other was from Ingrid, who said that our offer had been rejected. "The owner," she said, "received a higher offer."

Two weeks passed before I managed to convince myself that this was true. Soon afterward, I decided to confess to Brenda's colleague that, despite her numerous warnings, we'd attempted to buy a house in Bridgewater. I explained that after the walk-through we encountered the owner in the backyard, where he refused to acknowledge our greeting. Once he went inside, I added, he scowled at us from his kitchen window. I also told her that he gestured for us to leave with a flick of his hand. "Needless to say," I concluded, "we did not get the house." Brenda's colleague was outraged. She was hysterical. She did not sleep well, I suspected, for quite some time. I considered us even.

TRASH

They'd assumed we'd come for trouble but we only wanted trash. There wasn't much of it, not like there would have been if we were assigned to clean one of the parks or abandoned lots near our homes, but we were far from there, and the boys planning to harm us were not people we knew.

This was the fault of City Hall. Paul and I had applied for summer jobs like the rest of our teenage friends, but instead of sending us to work in South Shore, they'd sent us to work in South Chicago, across the color line. All of our co-workers were white. The supervisor was too. None of the teens had spoken to us, but they'd spoken about us, complaining loudly to one another that we had no right to be in their part of the city. Paul and I kept quiet. We remained a few feet from the group as it methodically moved through an open field, looking for garbage to harpoon; each of us carried a stick with a nail protruding from the tip. It had already occurred to me that these could be deadly weapons. I suspected it had occurred to the white boys too.

Their tempers seemed to rise with the late-June sun; mild complaints we'd heard at nine were vile epithets by noon. It must have been a hundred degrees by then, which couldn't have helped their dispositions, nor had they been helped by the consumption of beer. Thirty minutes earlier the supervisor had brought a case of Budweiser to the area of the park where we were to have our lunch break and sat it in the shade of a maple tree. The boys gathered around and started drinking. Paul and I sat nearby in the grass, roasting in the sun with our wilted bologna and cheese sandwiches. Our sticks were at our sides. We'd already agreed that if the name-calling threatened to give way to physical abuse, we'd hurl the weapons at them and run.

They hurled something first, an empty beer can. It landed a few feet from Paul. "There you go, *niggers*," yelled one of the boys. "Clean that shit up like you're supposed to." The other boys laughed, doubling over in stitches that made my blood boil. Another can flew our way, and then another, followed by more laughter that was cut short when my harpoon sailed through the air. It drifted wide left, just as Paul's did a second later. The white boys looked back and forth between our weapons and us, as if trying to comprehend what had happened. "Get them!" someone ordered, and in an instant we were all running at full speed, two hares and a pack of hounds.

We headed toward a strip of stores on Commercial Avenue, terrifying pedestrians and causing them to scatter. Now and then one of them cheered on our pursuers, but no one tried to stop us. And the white boys couldn't keep up. With each block their name-calling and threats grew more distant until at last their voices faded entirely. By the time Paul and I had the nerve to glance over our shoulders, no one was there. We slowed to a walk, but once we caught our breath we started to run again. It took us over an hour to get home. We spent some of that time crying.

Our parents were furious. They made phone calls and wrote letters, trying to get the supervisor fired and us reassigned to new job sites, all to no avail. Either we returned to South Chicago, they were told, or we lost our jobs. We did not return. By summer's end, all of our friends who had worked the whole three months strutted around cloaked head-to-toe with the latest fashions and pockets full of money. But Paul and I were not envious of these things. We only wished we'd had better aim.

TECHNICALITIES

*T*he house was an antique Colonial owned by a Republican law-
yer and a stay-at-home mom. I slowly turned onto the driveway
and pulled in—not too far, just enough to see a one-car garage in
need of repair and, deep in the expansive backyard, two enormous
boats docked for winter. I looked through the slider to my right.
The mom was sitting at the kitchen table, staring at me. She
waved unexpectedly, and I returned the gesture before reversing
out onto the street. I wrote down the phone number listed on the
FOR SALE sign and sped to our apartment, just a few blocks away.
After propping Adrian in front of *Sesame Street* with a cup of
Cheerios, I called and asked the selling price. It was a hundred
thousand more than Brenda and I could afford, a mere technicality.

We viewed it the next day. At the completion of the walk-
through, overwhelmed by the house's elegance, we could not
bring ourselves to leave, so Brenda and I lingered in the foyer to
chat with our real estate agent, Ingrid, while Adrian played on the
stairs. The stairs were covered with dirty beige carpet that, men-
tally, I had already removed. There would need to be some paint-
ing in the living room and study, and the roof and chimney were
in pretty bad shape. But there were large windows with great
southern exposure, high ceilings, built-in bookcases, hardwood

floors, and the spacious kitchen had new cherry cabinets. We were disappointed that there was no fireplace, but Ingrid explained that when the house was built, in 1896, oil-heating systems were all the rage; to *not* have a fireplace was a sign of prestige. It was an interesting fact, the kind I could see myself mentioning while giving friends a tour, though I would rather be entertaining them near crackling logs of pine.

We were discussing the asking price, which Ingrid felt was a steal. If the house was to be ours, she assured us, we must act soon. It had only been on the market for a day, just moments, perhaps, before I'd happened to drive by.

I asked Brenda what she thought. "I don't know," she responded, shaking her head. "I just don't know."

"I think we should make an offer *right now*." I turned to Ingrid, hoping she would agree. She had shown us houses for two months and obviously knew that this was the best of the lot. She knew, too, that we could not afford it. "Don't you think we should make an offer, Ingrid?"

The commission she stood to make was not enough to buy her soul. "It *is* a beautiful house," she said, "but maybe you should wait until you get a teaching position. I don't want you to end up in trouble."

But there would not be any trouble; all the pieces were in place. We just had to convince Brenda's mother to relocate from Chicago to help babysit Adrian and the newborn expected in June, and I had to be hired by the college. The first would be easy; Brenda's mother was about to retire and had no ties to the area that could compete with being near her only biological child. And getting the teaching position would be even easier. Bridgewater State College was looking for someone to teach African American literature and creative writing. It was not a done deal, but I felt the position was mine to lose.

"I'll get the position," I said confidently.

"I know you will," Brenda agreed.

Ingrid looked at her. "Then what's the problem?"

"The problem," Brenda replied, "is that Jerald doesn't *want* it."

Ingrid looked at me.

"A mere technicality," I said.

Later that night, after putting Adrian to bed, Brenda and I sat at the kitchen table. Before us was her hot chocolate, my cold beer, and a piece of paper with "Buy the House?" scribbled across the top. Just beneath that were "Pros" and "Cons." We spent the next hour filling in the two columns. When we were done, there were seventeen pros, and one con. But the one con was weighty: I did not want to teach. The pact Brenda and I had made was for her to teach while I watched the children and wrote, but that was operating under the dubious assumption that one faculty salary would be sufficient for us to acquire the things we needed; an assumption made with midwestern real estate in mind and perspectives shaped by lifetimes of poverty. When we had learned that Brenda's salary would be in the midforties, an incomprehensibly extravagant sum to us, we imagined ourselves owning a sprawling New England house, its swimming pool collecting leaves in the summer while we delighted in the sights of Rome.

But at that moment we were sitting in a cramped apartment listening to a neighbor bang on the wall. Adrian had started to cry a short while ago, and we had let him, trying to teach him to get himself back to sleep. The older man in the adjacent unit was urging us to try a different approach. Brenda went to Adrian's room. I called my mother.

"The house sounds very nice," she said. "But no fireplace?"

"I'm afraid not."

"Well, that's okay. You don't *need* a fireplace. Actually, you don't *need* an antique Colonial. Can't you find a less expensive, regular house?"

"We're in New England, Mom. Antique Colonials *are* regular

houses. Besides, it's the second least expensive house we've seen on the market since we've been here."

"Well," my mom continued, "if you want to continue writing, maybe now's not the time to buy a house."

"But we can barely even afford this apartment. Besides, Adrian needs a yard to play in."

"You mean you want a yard for Adrian to play in. You didn't have a yard to play in when you were his age. You lived in the projects then, remember? Don't forget where you came from."

But that was my problem—I could not forget where I had come from, despite spending my whole adult life trying to. Perhaps the purchase of an expensive, elegant house would trigger the amnesia I desired, blur the past enough to blunt its sharp edges. I imagined a moving truck backing toward the antique Colonial's rear door, not to deliver things, but to take things away. "That's a lot of stuff," the mover would say, surveying the poverty, bad schools, jails, guns, drug addictions, gangs, and murders. I am determined, I would explain, to shield my children from all of the things you see here. My children will live in safe middle-class communities. They will travel. They will have many opportunities to explore who they are, and who they might become. They will be advantaged. "So," the mover would say, "will you be paying for this with a check or cash?" I'd think about giving up my writing. I'll pay for it, I'd say, with a dream.

Brenda returned to the kitchen just as I was hanging up the phone.

"Who was that?" she asked, taking her seat at the table.

"My mom. I called her to say I'm applying for the position."

"You are?"

"Yes."

She inhaled deeply, her face full of concern. "You're not going to get much writing done teaching four classes a semester, you know, if any."

"I know."

"And you're okay with this?"

"Yes."

"Really?"

"Really."

She rose and hugged me. "You're lying," she whispered.

A mere technicality.

BREAK-IN

The house belonged to a middle-aged woman and her longtime boyfriend who drove a garbage truck. They had a daughter who was about ten, and you could already see that in a few years she'd be beautiful. I was in her room now. Above her bed were a life-sized poster of Michael Jackson and a Girl Scout certificate of achievement. I considered tearing them down but decided against it and joined Zack in the master bedroom, where he was ankle-deep in bras.

"What the hell are you doing?" I asked.

"I'm dumping the drawers."

"What for?"

"It's what burglars do," he said. "Protocol."

"Well, you're making a mess."

"What are you, the goddamn maid?"

I started dumping drawers. When a forty-five automatic fell to the floor, tangled in purple lace panties and a long strip of black ribbon, I picked it up and put it in an empty pillowcase. We dumped a few more drawers and found some jewelry, thin little necklaces as weightless as floss, which I put in the pillowcase too, and when there was nothing left to dump we went into the spare bedroom and dumped everything there.

A few minutes later we crawled out of the basement window we'd entered and ran to 79th Street. It was cold that morning, maybe in the low fifties. We blew into our cupped hands until the bus came.

Across from our stop, overlooking a favorite nightclub of prostitutes and ex-cons, was an apartment building on the verge of collapse. The back stairs creaked as we sprinted to the third floor, and the landing, rotted and sprinkled with cigarette butts and mouse shit, sank a little under our weight. We entered the dark hall and walked several feet, stopping at the unmarked door on the left. I knocked with an elaborate rhythm. A short while later, locks clicked, the door swung open, and Tim let us in.

We followed him into the living room and sat on a couch that smelled like sex and sour milk. The walls were covered from floor to ceiling with glossy pictures of naked women, torn from the stacks of *Hustler* and *Playboy* that lined the room like sandbags against a rising tide. There was an actual tide a block away, which I could see through the window, a stretch of Lake Michigan known as Rainbow Beach. Only four years earlier, when I was twelve, I swam in its greenish brown water, untroubled by the smell of raw sewage, or the shocked-looking trout whose dead bodies bobbed against the shore.

"So," Tim said, "whatcha got?"

We showed him our stuff. "We did pretty good," Zack bragged, "for our first break-in."

Tim agreed. He put the stuff back into the pillowcase and offered us ten dollars each. This was not a fair price, but being novices to the underworld and having limited connections, we took it. Zack put his share in his pocket and said he was going to visit his girlfriend. After he'd vanished into the hall I joked, enviously, that he was pussy-whipped. Tim grinned at me and asked, "Guess where I was when I first got some?"

I hunched my shoulders. "On this couch?"

"Gold Coast," he said, rubbing his chin. "Back when I stole

my first car." I settled into my seat as Tim began a tale of sex and car thievery while dividing up lines of coke on the glass coffee table. A mile away, one of my honors teachers was probably taking roll, pausing to shake his head, once more, when he reached my name.

THE INTERVIEW

I am a strong believer in the power of protest, and so within an hour of the incident I'd already completed a draft of my letter. I'd started it by explaining that my frequent patronage of this particular restaurant was due not only to the excellent food, but also to the exemplary service. The second paragraph was spent expressing my shock at the chef's rude insinuations, for which I was at a loss to contribute a motive, though I feared my race might have played a role. "I am a college professor," I said in closing, "not a lowdown sushi thief."

I wasn't actually a college professor, but rather in the process of trying to become one. Earlier that day I'd had my telephone interview with the English Department's search committee. I'd felt good about the interview at the time, but that feeling lasted for only thirty minutes. By then I was convinced I'd done poorly, which meant we'd lose our house, purchased only three months ago in December on the gamble that I'd be hired. I looked across the table at Brenda, now six months' pregnant, and shook my head. "I'm sorry," I mumbled for the dozenth time.

"You're being silly." She smiled at Adrian. "Is Daddy a silly willie?"

"Or," I asked him, reaching for my beer, "a loser boozer?"

Adrian was too busy eating a wonton to decide. There was an

array of Thai food before us, enough to feed an army or, hopefully, lift my spirits. An hour after the interview had ended, I ordered sixty dollars' worth of takeout. Now, while telling Brenda some of the responses I should have given the search committee, I nibbled my way through the various cartons of food, coming to a halt when I tasted the sushi. My chopsticks fell from my hand. "The rice," I announced, "is mushy."

"Really?"

"It's *awful!*"

Adrian took a piece and ate it without concern.

I sighed. "Can you believe this day?"

"Try the mango curry," Brenda said. "It's good."

"First a bad interview, now bad sushi."

"The miso soup is good, too."

"*What?*"

"The miso soup, it's good."

I tossed my hands in the air. "You don't get it, do you?"

Brenda rolled her eyes. "The *su*-shi," she said, "is *mu*-shi. I get it."

"But I really need it to not be mushy right now. It's inhibiting my emotional recovery."

"Perhaps there's some therapeutic value in chicken satay." She picked one up and bit it. "Mm! And it's tasty!"

I rose from the table.

"What are you doing?"

"I'm calling the restaurant to complain."

"Now you're being ridiculous."

The hostess did not agree. She apologized profusely and asked me to bring the mushy sushi back for a replacement. I collected the uneaten pieces and got my keys.

I jogged through the light rain to the restaurant's entrance, reaching it at the same time as a young man and woman. I held the door open before following them inside. The restaurant was crowded. Two-thirds of the twenty-odd tables were occupied. I scanned the room for people I knew, since many of our friends also dined there, but saw no one. I fell in line behind the young couple and eight other people. At the counter, the hostess studied her seating chart before leading a party of three to a table. She returned, greeted the next patrons, and then studied her chart some more. Behind her, the kitchen's double doors parted and a waitress emerged balancing a tray of steaming food. I watched her head for a table to my left, where a group of six smiled with anticipatory delight. Then it hit me, that odd sensation I often get of being watched. I looked toward the kitchen doors, where I saw, framed in one of the small, oval windows, a woman's face.

The door behind me opened. I glanced over my shoulder as two men entered with closed umbrellas, water dripping off the tips. I turned back toward the kitchen; the woman was still there, staring at me. The hostess seated two more people; the line moved forward. Waitresses darted in and out of the kitchen, requiring the woman to move, but by the time the doors had flapped to a rest, she was back again. Five people stood in front of me. Now two. I looked at the face in the window, and then I looked behind me, where the two men had started to argue in low voices, something about a used Mercedes. They had hung their umbrellas on the coatrack.

"Can I help you?" the hostess asked.

I turned around. The young couple was gone. I was next in line. I approached the hostess and sat my container on the counter. "I called about this . . ."

"The sushi?"

"Yes."

The hostess smiled, bowing slightly. "I'll replace it for you."

"Thank you."

She took the container and went toward the kitchen. The doors opened before she reached them, and the woman who had stood there emerged. The two women spoke for a few seconds in Japanese before coming to the counter.

"I'm chef," said the woman who had been staring at me. She took my sushi from the hostess. "What's wrong with sushi?"

I leaned forward and spoke quietly: "I'm afraid it's sort of mushy. The rice."

"Sushi rice supposed to be mushy."

"I know. But this is a little *too* mushy."

"It cannot be rolled unless mushy."

"Right. Yes. I understand, but . . ."

"You have sushi before?"

"Of course I have. My wife and I eat here all the time."

"Sushi rice *supposed* to be mushy, but I'll replace this once." She carried my container into the kitchen.

The hostess looked past me. "How many?" she asked the men. "Two?" One of the men said yes. She checked her seating chart before taking them away.

When the chef returned, she was holding the container I'd brought, as well as a new one. She plopped mine on the counter and pointed at it. "Sushi missing," she announced.

For a moment I thought she had meant that they were out of sushi, that it had vanished somehow, mysteriously gone away, and then I realized what she was saying. "Oh, yes," I said. "We ate two pieces."

"Why did you eat the sushi if mushy?"

"We didn't actually *eat* it," I explained. "We *tasted* it."

"Two pieces missing!" she said loudly, and I could hear the patrons' voices falling away.

"Wait a minute. Are you suggesting I *stole* the sushi?"

"Two pieces missing!" she snapped. "Next time, don't eat!"

"I didn't *eat* the sushi!" I said, my voice rising to match hers. "I *tasted* it!"

"Don't taste next time!"

"How will I know if it's mushy if I don't taste it?"

"Sushi is *supposed* to be mushy! If you don't like mushy rice, don't eat! Eat crispy noodles instead!"

The restaurant was quiet now. I looked toward the patrons. Everyone was looking in our direction, mouths agape. I looked at the chef. We stared at each other for an instant before she said, "Here new sushi! Take! Take! But *don't* come back!" She sat the container on the counter. I left it there.

On the drive home, I thought of the civil rights workers who had staged protests at lunch counters, putting their dignity, if not their lives, on the line for the right to be served. And here I was, a mere generation later, in no physical danger, my dignity bruised but intact, and my life not in jeopardy. *There is victory here,* I told myself.

But it was no use. Victory wasn't what I wanted. I wanted revenge. I would come back that night, I decided, dressed in an all-black outfit, my face hidden beneath a knit ski mask, and throw a brick through the goddamn window. I turned the car around, drove through the parking lot, considered the best escape route, and as I cruised home I decided to return at dawn and carry out the kind of act that would have made Malcolm X proud. Before Brenda or Adrian stirred, I would be back in bed, no worse for the wear. I thought of the cook's expression when she would arrive to see their window smashed to pieces, a brick resting where I had stood listening to her rant. The image caused me to smile, and all the way home I broke out into wild fits of laughter.

But a short while later, after discovering, to my relief, that I did not own an all-black outfit or a knit ski mask, I wrote a letter instead.

Three mornings later, the restaurant's owner called; he had received my complaint and wanted to talk in person at my earliest convenience. That moment, it seemed to me, was as convenient as any.

It was just after 3:00 PM. The restaurant was empty. Still, a waitress led Brenda, Adrian, and me to a far corner, where a screen had been placed near a table, shielding it from the rest of the room. Another waitress brought us ice water with lemon wedges. Brenda sat Adrian on her lap and began quietly reading *Green Eggs and Ham*. A moment later a pudgy white man approached us, followed closely by the chef. "Hello," he said, smiling. "I'm Jack, and this is my wife, Masako." They sat across from us. Jack was holding my letter. He looked at it for a long time before speaking. "This is very troubling," he said.

"Yes," I agreed.

"Tell me, please, exactly what happened."

I relayed the story. When I finished, his wife spoke. "I am not racist," she said.

"I'm not saying that you are," I responded. "I'm saying that I cannot think of a logical reason for your treatment of me. My race is a theory."

"It was busy. I was very busy. I might have had short temper. I apologize if my temper was short." That was all I needed to hear. I thanked her and started to rise, but stopped when she began speaking again. "I am not racist," she repeated. "I cannot be. You see, I'm minority, too. Japanese." I thought she would elaborate, but that was it, her complete defense summed up in her ethnicity. She grinned and went on the offensive. "*You* too sensitive. You came in very, very sensitive that night."

"I get very, very sensitive," I said, "when I am accused of stealing sushi."

"Do you know how difficult restaurant business is?" she continued. "Bad customers *all* the time." She described, then, some of the bad customer behavior, and the stories were amusing, until she singled out blacks. "They order takeout, bring it back half eaten, and demand refund."

Jack reached over and put his hand on her wrist. "Whites do this, too."

"But especially blacks," Masako said.

"*Everyone* does it," insisted Jack, now turning to scowl at her. He turned back to Brenda and me. "But that's beside the point. The bottom line is that all of our customers mean a great deal to us, and we hope you will continue your patronage." He reached into his breast pocket, removed a slip of paper, and placed it on the table between us. I leaned forward to see it better. It was a gift certificate for twenty-five dollars. When I picked it up, the chef nodded and smiled, confirming in her mind, perhaps, that this was what I'd wanted all along.

During the ride home I broke out into wild laughter again, as I sometimes would over the next few years when I thought of this incident, or happened upon the gift certificate. Even now I cannot help but chuckle as I imagine the chef, standing behind her kitchen's double doors, her stern face framed in one of the oval windows, waiting for my return.

BREAK-OUT

*T*he teacher patrolled the classroom looking over students' shoulders, frowning, shaking his head, making his way in my direction. I was hard at work, too busy protracting and compassing to respond when he asked me if I'd been drinking. He asked me again. I pressed my lips tight against a Jim Beam exhale. And then I belched. A large white hand snagged my wrist, causing me to draw a line even more crooked than the others.

I was jerked to my feet and pulled into the storage room, and who knows what would have happened if someone hadn't knocked on the half-closed door. We turned and saw a girl in a white blouse and a short blue skirt, bobby socks neatly folded on her greasy-looking shins. Her hand was raised and balled into a fist, poised to knock the door again but in the last instant was lowered and thrust forward, revealing two crumbled dollar bills. "Can I get some M&M's?" she asked. "With nuts?"

The storage room was full of them; crates upon crates that would help fund the girls' basketball team Mr. Harrison coached on the side. He opened one of the crates and removed a box of candy, exchanging it for the girl's money. While this was taking place, I noticed a ring of keys on one of the boxes. I slipped it into my pocket. As the girl turned to leave, Mr. Harrison faced me and said with great pity, "You're a fool." Then he made me leave.

When I arrived home, my mother was in the kitchen, washing a mountain of dishes. She didn't want to know why I was back from school so early. She didn't want to know anything. All of her hope for me was gone, and with it her anger, vanished into thin air with my immense potential.

I made a turkey and spicy mustard sandwich before going to my room. For the next eight hours I thumbed through magazines, napped, and watched TV. It wasn't until I was getting ready for bed that I remembered the keys. I glanced at my clock; it was almost eleven, not too late to call Tim, or anyone else, for that matter, whose livelihood was generated outside the law. He agreed to pick me up. A few minutes later, dressed in all-black and wearing a knit skullcap, I climbed out of my window and ran to his idling car. Motown thumped from the speakers as we drifted toward school.

He parked in back of the main building near a Dumpster overflowing with full garbage bags. Across the street, a fleet of bungalows loomed in the darkness. I opened my door. Tim didn't open his. He lit a joint, exhaling in my direction as he talked about his sore left knee and suspicions of car thieves in the area.

"Maybe you should wait here," I suggested.

"That's what I'm thinking."

"Got a flashlight?"

"It just so happens."

There were four keys. The third one I tried unlocked a service entrance not far from where the car was parked. I went straight to the home economics room on the second floor. The same key fit. There were maybe forty typewriters, Smith Coronas with long black electrical cords nearly as thick as sailor's rope. I spent the next half hour carrying twenty of them to the car. When I brought out the last one, my arms were rubber. Sweat ran down my face and neck. By the dull glow of a streetlight, I could see that my shirt was streaked with dirt and oil and spicy mustard. Tim started the engine and put the car in drive. As we started to pull away from the building, I told him to stop.

"What for?"

"M&M's."

"M&M's?"

"With nuts."

There were probably a hundred crates. I figured there must be a safe. I didn't mention the safe to Tim, only the candy, for which he said he had no use. As I climbed out of the car, we agreed to meet at his apartment in the morning.

The same key unlocked the door to the drafting room but not the storage room. None of the others worked either. There was an opened transom, though, and I climbed on a nearby table and squeezed my upper body through. A puff of musty air entered my nostrils, followed by the unlikely smell of perfume. I'd forgotten to bring the flashlight and it was too dark to see the floor, but without another thought I eased my legs over the transom, released my grip, and crashed down below. I lay still for a moment, stunned less from the fall than by the sudden realization that this would be my last day of high school.

When I tried to stand, my left ankle gave way in pain. It was broken, I figured, or at least severely sprained, and this knowledge fueled my determination the way a bloodied nose motivates a boxer. I struggled to one foot and rubbed my palms up and down the wall until I found and turned on the light switch. There were about fifty crates of the hard-shelled candy, many of them knocked over by my clumsy entry. I didn't see a safe, but rather, sitting on a metal file cabinet off in a corner, a shoe box, its lid slightly open and revealing a pile of money.

But when I rushed forward, I saw that I was wrong; the shoe box contained mainly candy receipts and other slips of paper.

I hobbled into the drafting room and, in accordance with protocol, started dumping things. I overturned stools and tables, scattered T-squares, bowled a chair into the wall, sent tiny pencil erasers sailing through the air like pink shrapnel. I found a piece of chalk and stood panting and sweaty at the blackboard, wanting to write something dark and vicious, a phrase of such memorable contemptuousness that wayward students would adopt it as their creed. But I put the chalk down and left, because the only word that came to mind was *fool.*

BAIT

Ned was a classicist from the back-woods of Mississippi. He always dressed very casually, "fashionably poor" I think it is called, with ripped jeans and open-toed sandals; T-shirts frayed and unraveling at the sleeves. This was his exact outfit that October of 2002, merely a month into my academic career, when he poked his head into my office and said, "We shouldn't have hired you."

I offered him a chair.

"No thanks," he said, stepping inside. He glanced at his watch and spoke quickly. "You clearly weren't the most qualified of the candidates for the position."

"So then tell me, Ned, why was I hired?"

"Your wife teaches here. And because of, well, another *obvious* reason."

He did not state the *obvious reason,* but it was fair to assume he was referring to my race. The minority faculty at the college numbered somewhere around 1 percent. I was the only black person in our department. I was, in fact, only the second black person my department had ever hired in its 165-year history. I may also have been the most qualified candidate for the position, but as long as affirmative action exists, whether or not it is actually applied, "best" is a distinction blacks will rarely be allowed to claim.

"Anyway," he went on, "the whole department knows you

shouldn't have been hired. I'm just the only person honest enough to tell you. That's also why I'm the only person who didn't vote for you."

"Well, I can't say that I blame you."

He raised his eyebrows. "You agree that you aren't qualified?"

"No," I said, "but I do agree that there might have been better fits."

"Really?"

"The ad expressed a preference for an Americanist. I'm an Interdisciplinarian." I leaned forward and whispered, "I may not have voted for me either." I sat back, loosening the knot of my tie. "Nevertheless, I'm here now, so we both may as well make the best of it. Besides, my students seem to enjoy my classes."

"I've heard. We share some of the same kids. They like you. They think you're great, actually."

"Which," I said, "raises an interesting question." I sat on the edge of my chair. "Knowing what you know now, that I'm not an awful teacher, and that I do seem to have a handle on the material, if you could do it all over again, would you vote for me?"

"No." He snickered and looked at his watch before disappearing into the hall. I was left feeling a mixture of confusion and anger, with anger gaining ground. I couldn't imagine what would motivate him to initiate such an exchange, particularly when a likely response would be a loss of temper. Now my conspiratorial mind was beginning to reel, and it didn't take me long to conclude that perhaps his intention all along had been to provoke me to some foolish response. It was the oldest trick in the book, one that I had fallen for often. One incident in particular came to mind.

It was 1980, and I was sixteen, crying, and in the back of a squad car. The cop sitting next to me was large, white, and male, standard for black ghettos at the time, and it is a peculiar trick of memory that I see him now with Ned's face. "You piece of shit!" he was yelling. "I could break your fucking neck!" It was a wonder he hadn't already. His hand was so tight on my throat that I could barely breathe. The nose of his revolver was pressed against my ribs. We were parked behind a police station, as reasonable a place as any for my murder. The officer no doubt would have claimed I had made an attempt for his gun, when, in actuality, I had only insulted his mother.

We had just arrived at the police station when it occurred. I was sitting next to my best friend Steve, who, like me, had been arrested for drinking in public and for truancy—it was 10:00 AM on a Monday. We should have been in school. But school was of little interest to me in those days; I had dedicated my life to the pursuit of trouble. I found it that morning in the company of winos. Steve and I stood with them in an alley, huddled in the shade of tenement stairs as we shared lies and a quart of Wild Irish Rose. The police appeared out of nowhere. Everyone was searched, but only Steve and I were handcuffed. We watched the officers empty the bottle onto the curb before walking us to the car. Behind us, I could hear the winos complaining.

"So, were you two niggers drinking *watermelon* wine?" was what started it all. I do not recall which cop said it, only that the other one laughed and responded in kind. They went back and forth, raising the ante at my and Steve's expense, and this was our entertainment during the entire fifteen-minute ride to the station, only I had found it less and less amusing so that, by the time we arrived, my anger was out of control. When one of the officers grabbed my arm and pulled me from the car, I looked him square in the eyes. "Your mother," I said, "is a *whore*." His face flashed red. He removed my handcuffs, pushed me back into the car, got in with me, and closed the door. It was not until he reached for his revolver that I understood what was happening.

And this is what saved me: Steve pounding his fists on the hood of the car, screaming like he was insane. The other cop grabbed his arms, trying to corral him, but Steve was too strong and kept breaking free. I could hear him yelling, "He didn't mean it! He didn't mean it!" and I wanted to join in, but I was being choked, and starting to cry. Police began to converge from all directions, nightsticks in hand, and while Steve was being clubbed into submission, the officer rammed his revolver into my gut before putting it away.

It is a vivid memory, its lesson clear, and yet I find myself too frequently that sixteen-year-old again, risking so much with so little to gain. I was lucky that day in the parking lot. And I was lucky that day in my office, that I did not take my colleague's bait. But the temptation was there, and that is what worries me. I have to be careful. I have to be smart. Steve can't save me now.

GREAT EXPECTATIONS

A guard came to the cell jangling keys and asked who had the blind father. The seven inmates looked around, fixing their attention on me when I raised my hand. "Get up!" the guard yelled. He inserted the key into the lock as I rose from where I'd sat on the floor. When I stood before him, he swung the gate open and asked, "So this is how you behave with a blind daddy?" It was a rhetorical question, apparently, because before I could answer he grabbed my arm and yanked me from the cell.

My father stood by the front desk holding his cane. The cane wasn't necessary, because he was with Tim, and I realized later he'd brought it only to play on the sympathies of the police. He never wore dark glasses, but I can now imagine him wearing a pair; anything that might have helped get my latest brush with the law—this time for a few joints of marijuana—swept under the rug. But the cane seemed to be working. "It must be difficult," the guard said, "being a handicapped parent, especially of a delinquent like this one."

"Oh, it is," my father replied, using a meek voice I'd never heard before. "It's difficult for my wife as well, who is blind, too, by the way. And diabetic."

My paperwork was discarded. I was released to my father's custody.

We piled into Tim's car with me in back. On the ride home, our father returned to being the man I'd expected, proud and stern, his voice straining with rage as he threatened to throw me out of the house, as he had Tim a year earlier, and Tommy a year before that. And in response I became the son he expected me to be, respectful of his authority, apologetic, my words barely above a whisper as I vowed to straighten up and get my life in order.

At home, I was sent to my room and told not to leave except for the kitchen or bathroom. It was only 2:00 PM. Eight hours later my father called me from the top of the stairs to make sure I was still there; after I responded I heard him lock the back door. Then there was creaking overhead as he moved through the living room to lock the front door too. I put away the magazine I held and got in bed with the full intention of sleeping, but when I was still awake an hour later I turned on my TV. There was nothing on I wanted to watch, so I dropped to the floor and did some push-ups. After that I did sit-ups and jumping jacks. I was doing deep knee bends when Greg's grinning face pressed against my window screen.

"What's up?" he asked.

"Not much," I whispered. "What's up with you?"

"We got some good weed," he said. "Me, Zack, and Louis." Over Greg's shoulder I saw legs and shoes, all but submerged in the darkness. "Come on out."

I thought of my father, how angry he had been, and I knew I needed to lay low for a while. "Naw," I said. "I'm cool."

"Come on, man. Just for a little while."

"I'm cool," I said.

"What you doing in there, reading again, like a white boy?"

I got dressed. After pushing a chair beneath the window, I hoisted myself up and climbed outside, because my friends, after all, had expectations too.

CAPTAIN WALKER

*F*rom my office window I watched a heavy snowfall, and it reminded me of a similar storm on the night of Greg's murder. He was the first of my childhood friends to die young, but we all expected to do the same. I was surprised when I reached twenty, amazed to see twenty-five. Then I was twenty-eight, thirty, thirty-five, and now forty, a college professor living far from Chicago's killing fields, but I still had not been able to shake the feeling that a violent, premature death was my due. And so I knew, long before Brenda suspected it, that one of my students intended to kill me.

His name was Sheng. I had met him four months earlier when he enrolled in my freshman composition course, though I do not know how he passed the placement exam because his writing was so poor. He was of Chinese descent and his accent was heavy, even though he'd been born and raised here in Massachusetts. I had pictured Boston's Chinatown when he told me this, even imagined him busing tables in some restaurant, above which an elderly aunt gazed pensively through her apartment window, remembering Beijing. But he lived in Easton with his mother. Easton was not particularly known for its Asian population. They may have been the only two—originally four, but his father abandoned them years ago, and his brother was dead.

"Tell me more," I said, "about your brother."

Sheng pointed the barrel of an index finger at his forehead, pulled the trigger. "Suicide," he said.

We were in my office, where he had accompanied me after the first class. My window was open and the clatter of the adjacent building's air conditioner made it difficult to hear. Closing the window was not an option, though, because there was no a/c in our building. The room's temperature had to be over one hundred. We were drenched in sweat.

"Twenty-three years old," Sheng continued. "A medical student. But he was under too much pressure. Success is very important to our mother. Maybe that's why our father left. He wasn't very successful." He looked at his watch, rose, and then picked up his backpack and slipped it over his frail shoulders. As he turned to leave, the pictures on my bookshelf caught his eye. He picked one up; it was of my family on the day of Dorian's birth. Brenda is holding him, and I am sitting next to her on the hospital bed with Adrian, then two, on my lap. I smiled as I recalled that extraordinary day, just three months before. I looked at Sheng; he was smiling, too. He asked me my sons' names. After I told him, he replaced the photo and asked, "Is success very important to you, Captain Walker?"

"Sure," I replied, "to an extent."

He smiled at me. "Captain Walker, did you get good grades in college?"

"Pretty good."

"You're very smart, Captain Walker."

"Sheng?"

"Yes, Captain Walker?"

"Why are you calling me that?"

"What?"

"Captain Walker."

"Because," he said with a grin, "you control my destiny."

.   .   .

Three weeks later I gave him a D on the first assignment, the lowest grade of the class. At the bottom of the page, I penned a note asking him to see me after class. I wanted to talk to him about ways he could improve his writing. He wanted to talk about trucks. "Does Adrian like eighteen-wheelers?" he had just asked me.

"Not particularly," I said, impressed by his thoughtfulness; he had remembered my older son's name after hearing it only once before.

"I'll bring him some trucks he'll like." Sheng opened his backpack and put in his paper. "Long red ones," he continued, nodding. "With little firemen inside. Little hoses."

Students from the next class began streaming into the room. I rose from my chair and stuffed papers in my briefcase. As Sheng and I walked toward the door, I mentioned his poor grade. "You didn't do very well," I told him. "Mainly grammatical errors, but there were some structural problems, too." He nodded. I suggested that he visit the writing studio. "They can help with some basics," I explained.

Sheng responded, "I'll bring you something chewy."

"I'm sorry?"

"Maybe a chewy rattle? Good for strong teeth. Does Dorian have teeth yet, Captain Walker?"

I laughed. "Sheng, he's barely three months old."

"I had teeth at birth. Six. My father gave me a chewy rattle. I don't know where my father is now, but I know where a chewy rattle is for Dorian. Maybe he'll have teeth soon."

"I don't need any trucks or rattles, Sheng, but I do need you to visit the writing studio."

"I will, Captain Walker."

"Good."

"Captain Walker?"

"Yes?"

He stared at me intently for several seconds. "To go to medical school, I need an *excellent* grade in your class."

"All the more reason," I responded, "to visit the writing studio."

If he followed this advice, it had no positive effect; his writing seemed to get worse instead of better. By the sixth week of class, it was clear to me that he would fail. That was also around the time he started following me. Several days a week, I would leave a class and find him waiting in the hall. As he escorted me to my next class or my office, we would chitchat about writing, his other courses, or the weather, but one day he mentioned his mother. She was in the hospital, he told me. I inquired about the nature of her illness. He said, "Whistling sounds."

"Whistling sounds?"

He whistled. "Like that."

"What about them?"

"She hears them all the time. But no one else can."

Early November arrived with the threat of a nor'easter. The first time I had heard this term was a year earlier, when we moved to New England. A weatherman issued dire warnings about its approach and I took him very seriously, having been born and raised in a city where the snow was a killer. Chicago's blizzard of 1978 took over one hundred lives, and one before that, in 1963, took sixty, including my uncle James, who had disappeared the night of the storm and was not found for three months, when the thaw exposed him facedown on a curb, missing a shoe. For twenty-five years, I was convinced that this was the world's worst weather, and then I moved to Iowa City where every spring tornadoes sent us fleeing to the basement in terror. After one direct hit to our town, Brenda and I walked the streets like war refugees, dazed and disoriented, stumbling over roof shingles and ducking beneath the roots of great trees. I had thought, then, of all the places I had never lived, and wondered what terrible meteorological deeds they had in store.

"Any idea what the weather is like in China?" I asked Sheng.

"Very good," he said, "if you like tsunamis."

We were being pushed along by a strong wind. For the first thirty minutes of my composition class, I had been glancing out the window and watching the skies grow darker and trees twist and turn, until finally I dismissed the students early so we could escape the storm. I had doubted I would make it across campus before the deluge, but after five minutes of brisk walking, accompanied as I so often was during that period by Sheng, I was still dry and my office building was just across the street, tucked within a sea of rippling ivy. Now, if I could just get rid of Sheng.

"I have to go to a meeting," I announced, "so I'll see you in class tomorrow." I looked at him to gauge his reaction, but it was impossible to see. He was wearing an enormous parka, the hood zipped to his nose, his face, from my side view, entirely concealed in a circle of fur, though it was fifty degrees outside.

"Captain Walker," he began, "do you like Chinese food?"

"Sure."

"Maybe Brenda likes it too?"

I had never told him her name. I stopped walking. So did he. For a second we just stood there, facing each other. "My mother is crazy," he continued, "but she's a good cook. I'll have her make something special for Brenda. Peking duck, only no duck. Too expensive. Maybe Brenda will like Peking chicken."

"Look, Sheng—"

"Can't talk now, Captain Walker. You have a meeting." He darted across the street, nearly being hit by a sedan.

My next class was not for another hour. I had gotten very little sleep the night before because both of my sons were sick, and so when I reached my office I closed and locked my door, pulled the shade, and settled in for a quick nap. I dreamed that I was dreaming, and when, in my dream, I woke and lifted my head from my desk, Sheng was sitting across from me reading a magazine. I forced myself awake. My heart was pounding. For a few seconds I did not know where I was, and then my surroundings began to make sense. I laughed out loud.

I laughed again that night when I told Brenda my dream. We had just put the boys to bed and were in our study, preparing the next day's classes. "This is getting ridiculous," she said.

"It's nothing."

"Nothing? You're *dreaming* about him."

"You don't dream about your students?"

She looked at me incredulously, still gullible, I thought, after all these years. I smiled. She frowned and said, "There's nothing funny about being stalked."

"There's something funny about everything."

"You need to tell the campus police."

I shook my head. "It's just Sheng."

"He could be dangerous."

By then I knew that he was. I knew, in my gut, that he wanted to kill me. "More needy," I said, "than dangerous."

She looked up from her computer. "How do you know that?"

"I just know."

"I've heard *that* before," she replied, and then she began telling me about some high school girlfriend and her deranged lover. I was happy when the phone rang and interrupted the story. *Let it be a real diversion,* I thought, *and not just a telemarketer.* I looked at the caller ID. My face, Brenda later told me, lost its color.

The conversation was brief. Sheng wanted to know if he was going to get an A. I told him no. I asked him not to call me at home. For two weeks he did not. He also did not attend classes. His mother had gotten worse, he explained when he did phone, and she needed his constant care, though I could not imagine what that could be. Perhaps he cupped her ears when the whistling started, or raised the volume on the television. I left assignments for him in a bin outside my office door, which he completed faithfully, but his writing did not improve. And he started calling me again. Each time his name appeared on the caller ID, I would pick up the receiver and settle it back on its base. It would ring again. I would let the answering machine get it. If he called back I would unplug the jack. One night, I had just completed this ritual and returned to the kitchen table when Brenda said, "If you don't notify the police, *I* will."

I moved my fork across my plate, gathering the last of my pasta.

"He's unstable."

"Maybe."

"He could *murder* you."

I did not reply.

"It's almost like . . . like you *want* him to."

I looked up from my food. "That's ridiculous."

"Then why don't you report him?"

"What's to report?" I asked. "He's just working through some problems."

"Apparently," she said, "so are you."

He called the next day and this time I picked up the phone. "You've *got* to stop this," I told him.

"We need to talk, Captain Walker. If you have a minute."

"I don't have a minute."

"Maybe you're putting Adrian and Dorian to bed?"

I did not answer.

"Or maybe you're washing dishes with Brenda?"

"What do you want, Sheng?"

"An excellent grade, Captain Walker."

"You're *not* getting an A. You'll be lucky to pass."

"We should talk about it some more."

I pinched the bridge of my nose. "Go ahead, Sheng. Talk."

"Not now. Tomorrow. In your office. One o'clock?"

"Fine, " I said. "One o'clock."

"It won't take long," he assured me. "Two minutes."

I hung up and went into the den. Brenda was reading. She looked up from her book. "Who called?" she asked.

I said, "My mom."

I had never wanted a physical barrier in my office between my students and me, and so soon after my hire I had pushed my desk to one side and placed a rocker in the center of the room. Sheng sat there now. The only thing separating us was his backpack, which rested at his feet. "I've tried my best," he was saying. "I've worked very, very hard."

"I know."

He squinted at me. "Maybe you don't know. You got good grades in school. It was easy for you."

"Nothing," I said, "was easy for me."

He lifted his backpack to his lap and let his hand rest on the zipper. I scooted to the edge of my chair. He released the zipper momentarily to scratch his chin. There was talking in the hall. I looked up to see three colleagues walking by, bundled up in hats and puffy coats. I glanced toward my window; snow rushed past as a nor'easter raged on, and here I thought of my friend Greg, of the fact that his murder, like the murder of any black male in the ghetto, was normal. But, I reminded myself, I was somewhere else now. I looked back at Sheng; he was staring intensely at Dorian's birthday picture, as he had the day we met, and I decided I wanted him out of my office. I said his name. He started to open his bag. I reached forward and stopped him, clutching a fistful of canvas.

"I have something for you."

"Just tell me what it is," I said.

"It's a surprise."

"I don't like surprises."

His body went slack, but he did not let go of the bag, and

neither did I. I asked him to put it on the floor. He reluctantly agreed. We lowered it together. I released it after him, and then, after a brief silence, asked about his mother.

He sighed deeply. "She wants money. I need a summer job. Can you get me a summer job, Captain Walker?"

I hesitated for a second, trying to formulate a distraction. "I think so. Maybe. Yes."

His eyes narrowed. "For real?"

"I think our counseling services can find one for you. If you explain your situation thoroughly. That means telling them everything you've told me: your mother's whistling sounds, your brother's suicide, your father, your anxiety about good grades, everything."

"This will get me a summer job?"

"Yes." Keeping an eye on his backpack, I found my campus directory beneath a pile of papers and dialed student counseling. When someone answered, I told her who I was and that I had a student with me who needed their services. I handed Sheng the phone. Their conversation lasted several minutes, Sheng becoming increasingly agitated, especially when talking about his mother. Just before hanging up, I heard him agree to go to their office, conveniently located in the same building as mine, if I would accompany him. "Ready?" I asked. He nodded and reached for his backpack, but I got to it first. Gesturing toward the door, I said, "After you."

The counseling services were tucked discreetly in a corner of the basement. We walked down the stairs and found the receptionist waiting for us in the hall. She led us to a small room with two couches and a table full of magazines. Before leaving she handed Sheng a clipboard with a form attached. He handed it to me. I read him the questions and wrote down his responses. A short while later, we were joined by the counselor, who was also of Chinese descent, a coincidence that seemed destined to work in our favor. She introduced herself, shook our hands, and then asked Sheng to follow her. He turned to me. "I see you later, Captain Walker," he said, and perhaps this is true. Perhaps one day I will walk into a classroom and see him in the front row, or as I wait in line in the cafeteria to pay for a sandwich, his hand will clutch my shoulder, or early some morning, when I enter my kitchen to make coffee, I will find him there. But so far I have not seen him since I left him with the counselor, who determined that he was an immediate threat to himself and to me. He was rushed to a nearby hospital for an emergency psychiatric evaluation. They admitted him against his will.

POOP

After telling me he'd stolen a car, Jimmy reached into his pocket and pulled out a roll of bills that, through the prism of my inebriation and poverty, I estimated to be five grand. He handed me a twenty and stuffed the rest in his pocket. "Me and my homey got two hundred each," he said. "Chopped up a Lincoln and sold the parts. I'm going to do it again tonight. Want to come?"

I did. I had developed a serious appetite for cocaine and, other than what money I got from petty thievery and selling a little pot now and then, I did not have a steady income. But I'd been drinking all day and was in no shape to go. I smoked some pot instead and went to bed early.

I dreamed I was in a subway station. My bed was in the center of the platform and crowds of people moved past me in streams. It was noisy and chaotic, terrible conditions for sleeping, so I decided to leave. I sat up and looked for the exit when a cop suddenly appeared before me. He said, "You're under arrest."

"Thank God," I responded. "Now maybe I can get some sleep."

"Okay, smart-ass. Put on your clothes."

The cop divided himself into two, and the subway morphed into my bedroom. There were strange things stacked along the walls: tires, a radio, bucket seats, and a steering wheel. I did a double take. I blinked hard. I wasn't dreaming anymore. This was real. "What the hell is going on here?" I asked.

One of the cops said, "You tell me, smart-ass." He dragged me from the bed. After I had gotten dressed, the other officer, dangling his cuffs on his forefinger, ordered me to turn around and cross my wrists behind my back. Cuffed, I was escorted from my bedroom and into the outer basement, where three more officers, my parents, Linda, and Jimmy were. Jimmy was in cuffs, too.

In the police wagon he grinned and said, "I stole another car."

I looked through the small window in the door. The sky was just starting to brighten. I figured it to be around five.

"It's in the garage," he continued. "And in your room. We were stripping it, and I guess somebody called the law. We must have been making too much noise."

I faced him. "Who's *we?*"

"Me and you."

"What? I didn't steal any car!"

"According to the police, you did."

"Who helped you?" I demanded to know.

"I'm not at liberty to say. But since the stuff's in your room, I guess the cops assumed you helped me. Obviously, I had to agree. There were eyewitness reports of two people."

I had stolen my first car while asleep. It was too much. "You have to tell them the truth," I insisted.

He was outraged. "Are you asking me to snitch?"

"Yes."

"I'm no snitch."

"Well, I'm no car thief!"

"That," Jimmy said, "will be very difficult to prove."

We were taken to a local precinct and placed in separate cells. It was a brand-new facility, the white walls unmarred by graffiti, unlike others that I had seen. The benches were made of steel instead of wood, and there was a toilet in the corner that I thought I would not use because of the surveillance camera overhead, but all bets were off twenty-four hours later.

Finally we were loaded onto a bus with a dozen other inmates and taken to another precinct. They held us in this one for several more hours, during which the guards laughed when I inquired about phone calls and lawyers. I began to think that somehow we had already been convicted and sentenced, but at last Jimmy and I went for a bail hearing. The courtroom was in the basement where, miraculously, our father and Tim were sitting in the front row. Jimmy and I were led directly to the judge's bench, which rose high in the air, in case our relationship to him was unclear. "Your bail's been posted," he said. After telling us our court date, he added, "Have a nice day." Just like that, we were free.

But our father arrested us again. No going outside until we went to court. No phone privileges. No allowance. No more living in his house without either a job or school. And no money for a lawyer. We had to use a public defender, a stocky, soft-spoken man who promised we would walk if we pleaded guilty. So that's what we did. The judge gave us probation, three years in which to screw up and have to face five-to-twenty. He rapped his gavel and said, "See you soon."

Jimmy had not dropped out of high school yet as I had, so I was the only one who needed to find a job. My father gave me two months. He could probably have given me a year and it wouldn't have mattered, since no one would hire me, not even Burger King or McDonald's. With a week left to go before he threw me out, my sister Mary, who'd returned from college and now worked at the medical center, told me she knew someone in human resources who might be able to get me a job.

"Doing what?"

"Cleaning test tubes."

"What's in them?" I asked.

She said, "Poop."

I did not like the direction my life was headed. And yet it felt right somehow, strangely on course, like bad things were supposed to happen to me and there was nothing I could do to stop them.

A PLACE OF REDEMPTION

*T*he author of the story being discussed must remain silent. The
work should speak for itself, I tell my students, though they often
fail to see the logic of this. "How can I not respond," they want to
know, "while I'm being criticized?" I tell them to bring something
to chew. A bullet, perhaps, or a stick. So far no one has followed
this advice. I have seen students pull hair, though, as well as bite
nails, grimace, crack knuckles, and even smile as it has been re-
ported death row inmates do at the moment of execution. But no
one had ever cried. That was about to change, I suspected, when
Diane walked into the room wearing sunglasses. She took her
usual seat to my right, but she did not engage in the usual chitchat
with the students near her, and they were not interested in
chitchatting with her. In fact, the whole room was eerily silent. I
looked at my watch. Six minutes to go.

Two more students arrived and quietly took their seats. Everyone seemed to have great interest in their hands, something deep
in their book bags, or in the manuscripts. There were three to be
discussed that day, and at this moment I cannot recall what the
other two were about. All I remember is that I discussed those
first, not to heighten the sense of drama, but because I did not
want Diane to have to sit through another hour of class in

emotional distress. This way, after her classmates filed out of the room, we could have the privacy we needed.

Her story was about a woman who could not conceive. Her gynecologist had told her this when she was twenty, which came to her as good news because she had no interest in being a mother. For the next fifteen years, she and her husband lived a blissful, contraception-free life, and then to everyone's surprise she got pregnant. She was angry with her doctor, her husband, and herself, but mostly she was angry with the baby. She referred to it as a "thing" and dreamed of snatching it unborn from her womb, only to be consumed by guilt when, at five months, nature snatched it for her. The story was well written, emotional, and full of the kind of specific detail that made me suspect that it was true. And then there was the fact that the author was in her thirties, like the main character, and both had been married for fifteen years. They both were nurses, smokers, and lived in the town of Newton. There was no doubt that the author had laid herself bare, led us to a car crash and pointed to her mangled body. She couldn't have known that mine was in there, too.

Just before I started the class, I reviewed my notes:

1) Never states why character did not want children. Give reason.

Brenda's was men. She had little faith in them when we met, thanks to living with an abusive father for sixteen years. Before the seventeenth year arrived, she and her mother filled a suitcase and slipped into the night. They were on the run for months, sleeping on the couches of friends. But he found them. "I'll never do it again," he promised, "if you just come home." He was evil *and* stupid. Trust him and a week later pieces of their limbs would be found mixed in the garden mulch. They did not go home. But they did not expect to live. Brenda had been expecting not to live for five years when I met her.

2) Husband very happy about pregnancy. Unclear whether or not he'd wanted a child all along. Was he depressed at the thought of not being a father? How had he felt when told of wife's infertility?

It took me two years to get Brenda to fully trust me, two more to get her to marry me, and another year to convince her that we should have a baby. As soon as she agreed, the first thing I did was buy books, three hundred dollars' worth of Dr. Seuss and Pooh.

"I shouldn't have bought books," I said. I was on the phone with my mother. Brenda and I had been trying to get pregnant for six months. "They were a jinx. And the cute outfits. The diapers, rattles, stroller—all of it. Jinxes."

"You're trying too hard," my mother said.

"How does one try too hard," I asked, "to have a baby?"

"Well, for one, those vitamins you told me about."

"The Mega Men's?"

"Yes," she said. "Stop taking those."

I couldn't. My sperm needed an edge. I'd watched a documentary about what they had to go through to reach the egg, a triathlon in miniature. I didn't want them panting as they crossed the finish line, or, God forbid, unable to finish at all. Extra-high doses of tryptophan was definitely the way to go. But even that wasn't getting it done. A year passed and still no luck. I stopped wearing underwear.

"Bad idea," Brenda said.

"Why?"

"It just is."

"The infertility book warned of excessive heat."

"You're probably exempt," she said, "since it's winter, in Iowa."

"Then what's wrong with me?"

"How do you know it's you? Maybe it's me."

"I knew it!" I said. "It's *you!*"

"I didn't *say* it's me. I said *maybe*."

"Well it sure as hell isn't me!"

"How do you know?"

"Tryptophan," I said.

We were quiet for a minute. Finally, Brenda said, "Maybe we should get checked."

The thought of doing so racked me with fear. What if my sperm weren't triathletes after all? What if they were fat little golfers, or couch potatoes? "Let's just keep trying," I suggested. The next day I bought a book with a title something like *Getting Pregnant Is a Cinch!* that guaranteed results in one month. All we needed were some charts, graphs, colored pencils, a thermometer, ovulation kits, latex gloves, cinnamon tea, and an hour a day for meditation. Five months later I threw away the book and my Mega Men's, along with my hopes of ever being a father.

Three weeks after that, Brenda was pregnant.

3) Very realistic how she doesn't suspect anything wrong when she can't feel the baby move for several days.

We checked our pregnancy books and read warnings about bleeding and cramping, but Brenda had experienced none of that. Just a small gush of liquid. We were fine. Totally okay. This was just the latest of the peculiar things, we told ourselves, that happen during a pregnancy. I called the hospital so they could agree. "How far along is she?" the nurse asked. I told her five months. She told me not to worry.

"That was odd," I said when I got off the phone.

"What?"

"She wanted our address."

"For their records probably."

A few minutes later we were surprised when two paramedics knocked on the front door. They chatted with us as they took Brenda's pulse and moved a stethoscope across her belly, inquiring if we were students and what our fields were. When they finished

the examination, they casually put away their things and told us
to go see her doctor.

My heart sank. "What for?"

"Observation."

"Are . . . are you taking us?" I asked.

"Oh, no, no, no. You can drive yourself."

I exhaled. "Thank *God*," I said, as if all hope rested in not riding in an ambulance.

"You had us pretty worried there," Brenda added. She placed
a hand on her stomach.

The paramedics went to the door. Before they left, one of
them turned and looked toward the couch, where Brenda and I
sat holding hands, and asked if this was our first pregnancy. We
told him yes. He wished us good luck.

*4) Doctor's coldness well rendered. Especially liked how he told
her baby had no heartbeat, and then said, "That's what you
get for not wanting it." Liked how she thinks of misdiagnosis
of infertility, toys with a lawsuit. All very believable.*

I was sitting in the waiting room near a screaming child and beneath a muted TV when an intern appeared, calling my name. "Better go to your wife," he said as I approached. "She's pretty upset."

"Upset? Why?"

"Obviously the miscarriage."

As if I had known. As if we'd just go home and try again, ignore the three years it had taken to get there. Ignore how close to
the due date we were, a stone's throw from viability. He was cold,
very cold, and no stories about vitamins, charts, ovulation kits,
and crying would warm him.

The intern said we could leave. Nature, he explained, would
complete the act without medical intervention. He asked me to
collect the remains for an examination. I asked to speak with him
in the hall. Once there I said, "Am I . . . is it . . ." I took a deep
breath. "What are we going to see?"

"Nothing."

"Nothing?"

"Just gray matter."

"Gray matter?"

"Pretty much."

"We're so far along, though. Five months."

"Nothing," he assured me, "will be recognizable." He got me a plastic, orange bucket.

Gray matter, I thought. Another peculiar thing.

5) Husband suddenly doesn't support wife, refuses to go to the surgery for D&C. Hard to believe his reaction. I concede, though, that stress can produce illogical behavior.

It seemed very important to me that Brenda have on her robe. But I could not find it. And I had to find it quickly because the paramedics were on the way. I ran back into the bathroom to ask her again. "Do you have *any* idea where you put it?" She did not respond, though, because she was unconscious. Her nude body lay in the tub, unmoving on a stream of bright red blood. The orange bucket was on the floor, full of the remains. It was not gray matter. The last two hours had been pretty intense. "I've looked everywhere," I said. I ran back into the bedroom and looked once more. Defeated, I returned to the bathroom and sat on the edge of the tub next to the thermometer, its mercury frozen at 105. I held my head in my bloody hands as my body quaked with sobs. "I just can't understand," I said, "how a bathrobe can vanish into thin air."

I remembered where it was! In the dryer! I went into the basement and looked, but it wasn't there, so I returned and resumed standing behind the paramedics, who had arrived a few minutes earlier and were hard at work. One of them was holding an oxygen mask on Brenda's face. Another was searching her arm for a place to put a very large needle. A third was yelling at her to wake up, to hold on. This was taking place on the bathroom floor. In my absence, they'd covered her naked body with a white sheet, which was okay but not nearly as nice as the robe I was searching for. Where could it be? I wondered. Where the hell could it be?

6) Guilt, rage masterfully captured; nice work.

I felt entirely responsible. In my youth I'd stolen, lied, used drugs, and blasphemed, completely drenched myself with bad karma. This was my fault, clearly. My just due.

For two months I was subject to bouts of guilt so debilitating that I could not bear to be in public. I especially avoided parks and malls, or any other place where I'd be forced to look away from babies. I looked away from the newly pregnant neighbor across the street. Then my sister Linda told me she was pregnant, so I looked away from her. I looked away from everything that should have made me happy. And then I got bitter, so I looked away from God, because, to my thinking, he'd looked away from me.

7) Powerful ending, very sad and intense. Very realistic that the marriage does not survive a trauma such as this. Her all-consuming depression is realistic, too. My only concern is that it may be too hopeless.

I was depressed for a year and a half. I did not even show signs of recovery when Brenda, after nine more months of trying, became pregnant again. I just could not convince myself to be hopeful. Certainly not about a baby being held in the womb by a string. Brenda had been diagnosed with an "incompetent cervix," meaning that if her cervix wasn't stitched closed during pregnancy, it would open once the fetus reached roughly twenty weeks of growth. Twenty-five weeks and it could survive with assistance. Thirty weeks and it could survive on its own. We made it to thirty-seven. And even with that, I wheeled her into the delivery room with low expectations. So I wasn't surprised when after forty minutes of labor the baby's heart rate suddenly started to fall. I knew it would stop completely. When it did, the alarm sounded, sending everyone into a wild panic, except for me. I fatalistically watched as triage carts were shoved into the room and more doctors ran in snapping on rubber gloves as they arrived. A nurse called the OR and screamed at them to get ready, and then the delivery doctor, with unnerving calm, said to Brenda, "We may have to have an emergency C-section. The baby's in trouble."

"Okay."

"But I want you to push one last time."

Brenda nodded.

"With the next contraction, I need you to push, push, as if the baby's life depends on it."

I knew that it did. Later, we would learn from the doctor that Brenda's had, too. I looked at the machine that monitored her contractions. The needle began to rise, wiggling toward its apex and then, after reaching it, holding steady.

"Push," the doctor said. *"Push!"*

Brenda pushed. I glanced at the baby's heart monitor. It remained blank. I looked at Brenda. Veins rose on her brow. *It's no use,* I wanted to tell her. *You're wasting your time.* But I knew she wouldn't believe me. I looked at the doctor. She was standing now, delicately working her forceps around what suddenly popped into view—a tiny little head! It was cone-shaped and covered in tufts of jet-black hair. The doctor praised Brenda, tugged some more, and a face emerged, silent and blue. Someone suctioned his nose and mouth before his limp body tumbled into the doctor's hands. A nurse grabbed him and ran to the corner of the room and placed him on a small table beneath a heat lamp. A team of medical staff converged on him; another converged on Brenda. "You did a *phenomenal* job," they told her. "You did *really* well." But there was no mention of the baby. I stood there silently, ignoring the full horror of what was happening, begging him to breathe.

8) After class, tell Diane what happened. Let her know that the baby survived and is doing well, and that he now has a little brother; were I to write a story about my experiences trying to become a parent, I would end it here. I'm not suggesting that stories have to have happy endings to be effective, but the enduring stories are the ones that are in some way affirmative, that can find something instructive to say about how and why to live. Maybe stick with the story a little farther, follow your character until she finds, like I found, a place of redemption, even if the redemption isn't in the form of a child.

GANG LIFE

*P*aul and I sat on his porch and drank red wine until the thought of what we were about to do failed to give us shivers. I poked my lobe once, just barely breaking the skin, and then slid the needle back on the spool of thread. I had not drunk enough. I doubted I could. I suggested we get some ice to numb our ears. "That," Paul said, "is an excellent idea."

He went into the house. I took another drink, wiping my mouth with the back of my trembling hand as I scanned our expanse of ghetto. Four girls played double Dutch off to my left, their feet eluding the rope with incomprehensible ease, while across the street Mrs. Wheeler knelt in her garden bed, tending to her peonies, pausing now and then to look pitifully in my direction. Balls bounced and children shrieked somewhere out of view. The screen door snapped shut. I turned around. Paul's hands were empty. "No ice," he said. I reached for the wine. We passed it back and forth until it was gone. I tossed the bottle behind the bushes and picked up my needle.

Ten minutes later, with black thread looped through our swollen earlobes, we stumbled to the park to proudly show some of the El Ruken generals what we had done. They congratulated us for joining their gang. Someone asked us our ages. We were seventeen. One of them told us to start lifting weights. "Can't whoop no Disciples," he warned us, "with skinny-ass arms like those." They flashed us the gang sign—the left hand cupped on the back of the right—and after Paul and I returned the gesture, we went home and did push-ups until we were sober.

Gang life was good. Girls suddenly dug me, especially once I got the money for an actual earring, and boys respected me who had not before. I was invited to all the right parties; requests for simple favors were not refused. I even enjoyed my first gang fight, although it was only with Jimmy. He had, for some reason, started hanging out with a few Vice Lords, and one night, when we were both high, we showed each other where our loyalties lay. He busted my lip, I blackened his eye, but within a week we were at peace again.

Then some crazy stuff started happening with the Disciples. Carloads of them were seen cruising the neighborhood in search of rival gangs to harm. They found some, too. Stories of broken bones reached me every day. There was talk of a coming turf war. I started keeping a pair of brass knuckles in my back pocket, as well as a container of Mace in case I got in serious trouble. But then guns started being used and I surprised myself: I lacked the courage to either kill or die. I decided that my gang days were over. I tried to explain that to some of the generals when they offered me a .22.

"You kidding," one of them responded.

I shook my head. "I'm serious. I'm done."

"No, no, no," he said. "I wasn't asking if you were kidding. I was telling you. You can't quit. There's a war coming."

"But, but," I pleaded, "I'm on probation."

"Nigger," he said, *"we all on probation!"*

I took the gun. But I knew I would not use it. They must have known it, too, because later that night someone shot a bullet through our living room window. And the day after that, when a Chevy screeched to a halt at my side, I was not surprised that the six thugs who jumped out to chase me were from my own gang.

The El Rukens had declared open season on me, and on my twin brother, too. We began traveling through alleys or only at night. Sometimes they still found us, though, and the beatings we took were severe. Jimmy got a gun, a .45 that could stop a charging bear, while I started dating a girl who lived on the other side of town. She wasn't very pretty but she had her own place. She was agreeable to letting me stay.

"You're *running*?" Jimmy asked me when I told him.

"*Hell* no." I was dumping clothes into a garbage bag.

"I can't believe you're letting them punk you like that!"

"I'm . . . I'm not."

Jimmy shook his head. We stood toe-to-toe for a few seconds, not speaking. Finally he said, "And you call yourself a *gangster*."

"I am," I insisted. I pointed to my pierced ear, but it was an empty gesture. I'd already shown him my heart.

VISIBLE MAN

A fellow black colleague called me to her office and asked why I had not attended the Kwanzaa celebration. As a recently hired professor, I told her, I was overwhelmed, weighted down with responsibility and pressure, and in addition my two young sons were frequently ill, requiring a great deal of attention. But I was lying.

The truth is that I do not observe Kwanzaa. I recognize that the desire to celebrate customs and traditions is a good one, but Kwanzaa's emphasis on Africa simply has no personal appeal to me. I am American, not African. I speak English, not Swahili. I wear Western-style clothes intended for commoners, not kente cloth intended for royalty. I have no need to participate in a highly ritualistic holiday in order to feel better about myself; for that, my ancestors gave me Br'er Rabbit and John Henry. These were the remarkable Americans who invented spirituals, blues, and jazz. In no small part, they invented America, too.

I did not have the courage to say that. I had only been an academic for a short while, but I'd followed the profession long enough to know what happened to black faculty labeled "conservative." And somehow, not celebrating Kwanzaa would earn me that distinction.

My colleague leaned back in her chair, a frown thinning her lips as she looked toward the ceiling. I glanced up, expecting to see something perilous, a protrusion of water-stained plaster, perhaps, or a light fixture teetering from a single screw, but there was nothing of the sort, just a few harmless cobwebs wafting in a draft. "Racism in academe," she began, "is rampant. It's a disease. A cancer. An *epidemic*. As a person of color, I've had my share of battles." She shook her head sadly and said, "I tell you, there are some *seriously* misguided white folks around here. Black ones, too." She rested her elbows on the arms of her chair. "But there are also some *good people* in academe, there are some *good people* here at this college. It's important that these people—and they're good people, really, they are—see you at campus events, especially those that celebrate *our* culture."

I nodded. "Well, you know, I'd like to attend more events, all sorts of events, but I'm just so overwhelmed right now. It's difficult to stay afloat."

"I understand that. But you're one of a small number of black faculty on this campus, and, well, there are certain expectations there." She leaned forward. "It's in your best interest, particularly at this early stage of your career, to be more *visible*."

"I'll do what I can," I said.

"Don't be a disappointment."

"Of course not."

"Then you and Brenda will be at the Martin Luther King breakfast?"

I decided not to tell her I had already purchased tickets. "Yes," I said. "I'll make arrangements immediately."

"Good!" she responded, now smiling, and yet, somehow, still managing to look troubled.

The breakfast crowd was overflowing. It was easily the largest gathering of minorities I'd seen since we'd relocated to this overwhelmingly white town, and I wondered if, in the true spirit of King, they'd been bused in. There was a strong showing of the administration, including our black president, but there were at best only two dozen white faculty and staff. The rest of the attendees were hundreds of extremely well-dressed blacks, many of them surveying the room and smiling, pleased, in a way that only blacks can be pleased, to be at a large gathering of successful peers.

Breakfast was served buffet-style. Brenda and I were joined at our table by an elderly black couple, both of whom were retired faculty of a local college, and together we enjoyed a wide-ranging menu that included asparagus quiche and grits. After breakfast, the president said a few words, and then the keynote speaker took the podium. I do not recall exactly what was said, but I remember somber references to the lack of advances minorities have made since King's ultimate sacrifice. By the time the speaker finished, a palpable anger filled the room, for which he was given a rousing ovation. I applauded, too, even though I knew blacks had accomplished more in the last forty years than in the previous four hundred. I told myself that had King been alive, he would have preached this message instead, and I raised my guava juice to him in silent tribute.

In January, Brenda and I attended a few more high-profile events, and a couple of low-profile ones for good measure. February, Black History Month, kept us in high demand, and then things were quiet until early May, when I received an e-mail from the black colleague who had chastised me about not attending Kwanzaa, reminding me of the approaching Kente Cloth Ceremony, aka "Black Commencement." I knew that it, like Kwanzaa, would be largely African-themed, but that was not what concerned me most. What concerned me most was that, after so recently celebrating our country's staunchest promoter of integration, I was being asked to celebrate segregation, to teach our students, in essence, to derive meaning from their race, which King preached was our most meaningless trait of all. This is what I was thinking as I typed my RSVP, saying, cowardly, that I would be delighted to attend.

The next Saturday morning Brenda and I sat with the families and friends of students of color as they marched across a stage to receive the kente cloth they would wear during graduation. Candles were lit at various points of the ceremony to symbolize universal values, here described as "African," such as the importance of family, community, and faith. Poems were read. Libations were poured. Women wearing spandex beneath thatched skirts danced to the rhythm of beating drums, summoning ancestral spirits from across the Atlantic.

Later, after breakfast, the guest speaker, a black American, though with an African-sounding name, was introduced. He wore a wrinkled, double-breasted white suit, and dragged an enormous duffel bag to the stage. He had the longest dreadlocks I'd ever seen and, perhaps following some little-known custom, had buttoned them inside the front of his suit jacket so that they emerged beneath the hem, continued past his knees, and swept the tops of his white shoes as he moved. His lecture included references to ancient Egypt, Allah, mathematics, Imhotep, slavery, reparations, and cloning. He laughed, he cried, he sang; he removed large homemade instruments from his duffel bag and played songs designed to amuse children, though few were there. At some point I glanced at Brenda, whose mouth and eyes were wide open, and then I scanned the room and saw similar expressions of disbelief, including on the faces of the event organizers and the colleague who had invited me. It was a truly bizarre performance, the product of a madman, it seemed, and I decided, while watching him, to be a madman, too.

I would attend no more kente cloth breakfasts. I would not attend Kwanzaa celebrations. Never again would I applaud speeches that celebrated the myth of black defeat, and I would not participate in events simply because of the color of my skin. And if people questioned my absence, I would not tell them a lie. I intend to be visible, I would tell them, but only in ways I wish to be seen.

NAKED

I was waiting for the bus when a car drove past, the driver bobbing his head to his radio, his thumbs keeping time against the steering wheel, his body as naked as the day he was born. The two other people standing near me—a man with a bulky metal leg brace, and a teenage boy who was smoking one of my cigarettes—either hadn't noticed or weren't letting on that they had. I tossed the butt of my Newport to the curb and watched the car until it was out of view, wondering what would make a person do such a thing.

When I arrived at work, I didn't immediately tell anyone about what I had seen because, being one of only three blacks in my department, I tried to keep to myself. The other two blacks were my boss and a woman with bluish hair who hadn't spoken to me during the year I had been there. She was one of the hematologists—that was a new word for me when I started at the medical center, and the Department of Hematology was a new place: a large room full of rectangular tables covered with microscopes. All day and night hematologists stared into these microscopes, and sometimes I wondered what it was that they saw. I could have asked them this if I'd wanted to, because the hematologists were nice people, which is to say they smiled or said hello whenever we met, except for the black woman, who looked the other way.

My job was to clean the test tubes and beakers. I'd scrub them with a wire brush before putting them in the washer, and then wheel my cart to the ten small labs on the ward to collect some more. Most of the beakers contained human waste, so it was important that I wore my thick rubber gloves. I also wore a white knee-length smock, just like the hematologists, but I worked alone in a small back room that was so cold I had to wear long underwear beneath my clothes. There was a door that led to the back stairs, so I could sneak in and out when I didn't feel like dealing with any of the hematologists, which was pretty much every day. I just didn't have much to say to them, and they liked to ask questions about my personal life, things I didn't want to answer.

Three hours into my shift I went to see my boss. When I walked into his office he smiled and said, "Hey, what's happening, young man?"

"Good morning, Doc," I said. "How are you doing?"

"I'm making it, my man. I'm making it." He motioned for me to sit in a wingback leather chair that was as comfortable as stone and made me wonder if rich black people knew what to do with their money. "So," he said, "how can I help you?"

I started telling him about the naked man but the phone rang before I got very far. He excused himself and began a conversation with someone about spleens. I sat there for several minutes looking at all the books and journals that bowed the wall-to-wall shelves, and suddenly I remembered that I used to like to read. Another moment passed, and then another, until I'd sat there for five minutes. As I rose to leave, I decided to come back later, maybe during my lunch break.

But I didn't go back later. When my lunch break came I got my sandwich from my locker and went to the men's room. I sat in the stall farthest from the entrance and ate quickly because there's nothing worse than having some hematologist shitting next to you when you're trying to enjoy your tuna.

After I finished eating there were still fifty minutes to kill. I used them searching for Stan. Stan worked for the Food Services Department. All day he delivered meals to the units and dope to many of the employees. I found him on the oncology floor unloading plates of turkey and dressing. After I whispered what I wanted, he told me to give him half a minute, so I waited for him by the nurses' station near a unit clerk who was laughing into her phone. There was a wad of chocolate cake in front of her, and every few seconds she pinched off a clump and pushed it between her lips. This was the job I hoped to get someday. I had done a little research and learned that, of all the nonprofessional positions, unit clerk paid the most. Besides, the clerks had access to the prescription pads and doctors' narcotics numbers. I was looking forward to getting my hands on those.

Stan came out a few minutes later. We took the stairs to the first floor before leaving the building through the emergency room exit. It was late August. A strong humid breeze tried to keep us from crossing the street and entering the park. The trees had already started losing their leaves, and the ones we were walking through were wet, even though it hadn't rained.

We stopped near a bronze sculpture of an Indian on horseback. Stan handed me a gram of coke wrapped in a small scrap of newspaper. I handed him five twenties. As he was putting the money in his wallet, I told him about the naked man. He told me he would have kicked his ass.

"For what?" I asked.

"For being naked."

"What do you care?"

"I don't like seeing naked people driving cars. But I guess you do."

I denied this. "I'm just curious, you know, about his motive. I mean, what's the point?"

"The point," Stan said, "is to get his ass kicked."

I walked away knowing he was wrong. This wasn't about ass-kicking, or really even about nudity. This had something to do with confidence and nerve. This, it occurred to me, was about not working alone in a small back room, or eating your tuna sandwich in a bathroom stall.

GAME

After expressing concern that his puppies would develop racist tendencies for lack of exposure to minorities, a faculty colleague asked if he could bring the dogs to my house to play with Dorian and Adrian, who were, at the time, one and three years old. I declined the request. "My boys are afraid of dogs," I explained. If he knew of any racially deprived felines, I told him, he should let me know.

When I casually mentioned this exchange to minority faculty, some of them retold it to me, only now with themselves in my shoes performing a number of aggressive acts against my colleague. The white faculty I told did not put themselves in my shoes. Many accused me of lying. That's because the puppies' owner decided to deny—vehemently—that our conversation had ever taken place. To remind him that it had, I taped to my office door a photograph from the 1960s civil rights movement: a black male leaning just beyond the reach of a German shepherd that's being restrained by a white police officer. Right beneath the photograph I'd written: "Don't let this happen to you. Teach your dogs racial sensitivity."

"Was *that* necessary?" an administrator asked me.

I assured her it was.

About a month after I was told of the segregated puppies, I

had another interesting encounter with a different white colleague, this time while in the corridor outside my office. "Off to
the pool?" I had inquired, motioning toward his large duffel bag.
He was a thin man, very fit looking. I had taken him to be a swim-
mer.

"Basketball," he corrected me.

"Oh? Where do you play?"

"Over in the campus gym."

"Open shoot-around," I asked, "or is there a league?"

"Actually, some of the faculty get together a few times a week
to play."

I nodded and wished him a good game. He thanked me and
walked away. I went into my office and sat at the computer. When
I looked up a moment later, he was standing at my door.

"I *would* have invited you to play, I just didn't . . . um . . . get
around to it."

Before I could respond, he left again. But he came right back.
"I didn't even know whether or not you played."

I smiled and said, "I'm a black male from Chicago's inner city.
Of course *I got game!*" Actually, I did not have game. From the age
of five, I had failed to make every basketball team I had ever tried
out for, except the teen league run by my church, which had a
benevolent, no-cut policy. But I had always wanted to say *I got
game!* to someone who might believe me.

Red in the face now, he again hurried away. I waited for him
to return. When he did, he looked pretty shaken up. He apologized.

"For?" I asked.

"Well, it's just that I *wanted* to ask you to play, but I didn't
want you to think I'd singled you out because you're black. That
could be considered racist."

"True," I said. "But it could also be considered racist *not* to ask
me because I'm black."

"You're right, you're right." He lowered and shook his head, then looked up again. "I've just felt awful every time I see you. I feel awful even talking with you about it now." But he should not have. When blacks integrate predominantly white institutions like academia, racial incidents are bound to occur, but they are almost always sparked by innocent gaffes rather than ill will. My colleague with the puppies wasn't being racist when he made his request; he was, in his own unique way, simply trying to befriend me. Things got a little tricky when, instead of just admitting this, he accused me of fabricating our encounter. And that's why I so appreciated the second incident, for this colleague's honesty resulted in an open conversation about race. After we were done talking, I put no photograph on my door. Instead, I went to the campus gym.

There were a dozen white men already there when I arrived, most of them, I was pleased to see, feeble looking and elderly. As I approached the court, I shot an imaginary ball toward the basket. "Let's see who in here's *got some game!*" I yelled, and then I proceeded to be trounced. While I lay on the floor trying to breathe, I received looks from the players that seemed to be a mixture of suspicion and curiosity, as if I were some kind of fraud, not the genuine article. I had seen this look in academia many times before.

The first time was from my college roommate Lenny. He had spent the first eighteen years of his life in rural farmland so removed from integration that he had never met a black person before I walked into our dorm room. He confessed this several months later, but I had surmised it right off, based on the way his eyes widened when he first saw me, the panicky quiver in his voice when he told me his name, and how he had sat on his bed very quietly watching me unpack.

Things were strained at first. Lenny was nervous in my presence, while I, on the other hand, did not want to be in a dorm room with a nervous white farmer. But in time Lenny and I learned to accept our differences and each other, so much so that one night, three months into our four-month cohabitation, a few bottles into a six-pack of beer, he said, "You're the first colored person I've ever known."

"I prefer *black*," I said, "to *colored*."

"You do?"

I nodded. "But that's not true for all of us. Some of us like to be called African American. Negro was popular for a while, but not so much these days. I'm thinking of bringing it back."

"See?" Lenny said sadly. "That's what I mean. I don't know *anything* about the colored race." Lenny was sitting on his bed and I was sitting on mine. They were positioned like an *L,* only mine was high in the air, resting on stilts. The beds had been stacked one directly above the other, but neither of us had felt comfortable with that. "I was a little afraid of you at first," he confessed. "I mean, I didn't think you were a murderer or anything. I'd just been told that colored people were, you know, *different* from white people."

"How so?"

"Well, that you love fried chicken."

I laughed. "And watermelon?"

"Yes!" He laughed too before adding, "And that you have little tails."

"*Pardon?*"

"Little tails." He held up his hands, maybe a foot apart. Neither of us spoke for a long time. And then, almost inaudibly, he asked, "Is it true?"

I climbed down from my bed and mooned him.

"Was *that* called for?" he asked.

I assured him it was.

Or so it seemed at the time. But not long afterward, I came to understand that it was not my best moment, just as I have come to see that putting the photograph on my office door was not either. Both my college roommate and my faculty colleague were groping their way toward racial understanding, and if I could have contained my frustration a little better, I might have been a more effective escort as they made their important journey. But I am on this important journey, too. We all are. And in those instances when we veer from the correct path, when we momentarily lose our way, the thing to do is to admit it, to speak truthfully about our imperfections and failings, rather than to pretend they do not exist. In other words, when dealing with the complicated issue of race, shouting "I got game!" will take you only so far.

THE PROFESSOR

When I arrived at the lab there was a huge batch of dirty beakers and test tubes waiting for me, and I wished the medical transcription course I was taking was already finished. I had only three more weeks before I received a certificate that said I could transcribe doctors' orders, even though it was a skill that required no brain. I doubted some of my classmates could even read. My instructor must have doubted it too. He'd nicknamed me "The Professor" and was always calling on me to answer questions; once, when the class was on break and I was in the bathroom eating a Snickers, he started talking to me from the adjacent stall about college.

"That you, Professor?" he'd asked, even though he knew it had to be me; I was the only male student in the class. I got angry at myself for not making sure I was alone. When it occurred to me that he might have heard my candy wrapper, I started to sweat a little. My mouth was suddenly too rigid to move. For a few seconds, I couldn't speak or chew.

"Tell me something, Professor. How old are you?"

I opened my mouth and pushed the answer past my Snickers: "Nineteen."

"And why are you taking this course?"

"To get a certificate that says I can transcribe doctors' orders."

"Right. But why?"

"To get a job transcribing doctors' orders."

"I understand that," he said. "But you're pretty bright, as is evident by the way you're evading my questions. It just seems that maybe you should set your sights a little higher. Maybe go to college."

"I am in college."

"This isn't college."

"Yes it is," I responded. "It's Medical World Technical College. Says so right on the classroom door."

He ignored this, asking, "Any reason why you don't?"

I didn't answer.

"If money's the reason, there are grants and loans. And scholarships. I'll be happy to help you look into it. What do you say?"

I declined his offer.

He was silent for a while, and then he asked, "What are you eating?"

"Snickers," I said.

"Sounds good. Might have one myself."

It took me two weeks before I could look him in the face after that because it's an embarrassing thing to be caught eating a Snickers while you're on the toilet, but when we did make eye contact he didn't mention it. He didn't mention college either. Neither did I. College just didn't seem to be for me, even though I knew I was as smart as the hematologists I worked with. Sometimes, while I scrubbed the test tubes and beakers, I could hear them next door talking about politics, one of my favorite subjects, and the things they said usually didn't make much sense. A few times I'd nearly gone in there to join the conversation. Instead, I argued with them right there at my sink, quietly making point after point, none of which, I was sure, they would have been able to refute. But that wouldn't have been their fault. They were only hematologists. I was The Professor.

DRAGON SLAYERS

I was at a Christmas party with a man who wanted me to hate him. I should hate *all* whites, he felt, for what they had done to me. I thought hard about what whites had done to me. I was forty, old enough to have accumulated a few unpleasant racial encounters, but nothing of any significance came to mind. The man was astonished at this response. "How about *slavery?*" he asked. I explained, as politely as I could, that I had not been a slave. "But you *feel* its effects," he snapped. "Racism, discrimination, and prejudice will *always* be a problem for you in this country. White people," he insisted, "are your *oppressors.*" I glanced around the room, just as one of my oppressors happened by. She was holding a tray of canapés. She offered me one. I asked the man if, as a form of reparations, I should take two.

It was midway through my third year in academe. I had survived mountains of papers, apathetic students, cantankerous colleagues, boring meetings, sleep deprivation, and two stalkers, and now I was up against a man who had been mysteriously transported from 1962. He even looked the part, with lavish sideburns and solid, black-rimmed glasses. He wasn't an academic, but rather the spouse of one. In fact, he had no job at all, a dual act of defiance, he felt, against a patriarchal and capitalistic society. He was a fun person to talk with, especially if, like me, you enjoyed driving white liberals up the wall. And the surest way to do that, if you were black, was to deny them the chance to pity you.

He'd spotted me thirty minutes earlier while I stood alone at the dining room table, grazing on various appetizers. Brenda had drifted off somewhere, and the room buzzed with pockets of conversation and laughter. The man joined me. I accepted his offer of a gin and tonic. We talked local politics for a moment, or rather he talked and I listened, because it wasn't something I knew much about, before moving on to the Patriots, our kids, and finally my classes. He was particularly interested in my African American literature course. "Did you have any black students?" he inquired.

"We started with two," I said, "but ended with twenty-eight." I let his puzzled expression linger until I'd eaten a stuffed mushroom. "Everyone who takes the course has to agree to be black for the duration of the semester."

"Really?" he asked, laughing. "What do they do, smear their faces with burnt cork?"

"Not a bad idea," I said. "But for now, they simply have to think like blacks, but in a way different from what they probably expect." I told him that black literature is often approached as a record of oppression, but that my students don't focus on white cruelty but rather its flip side: black courage. "After all," I continued, "slaves and their immediate descendants were by and large heroic, not pathetic, or I wouldn't be standing here."

The man was outraged. "You're letting whites off the hook," he said. "You're absolving them of responsibility, of the obligation to atone for past and present wrongs . . ." He went on in this vein for a good while, and I am pleased to say that I goaded him until he stormed across the room and stood with his wife who, after he'd spoken with her, glanced in my direction to see, no doubt, a traitor to the black race. That was unfortunate. I'd like to think I betray whites, too.

More precisely it's the belief that blacks are primarily victims that I betray, a common view held by both races. I, too, held it for many years, before my workshop with James Alan McPherson. I knew when I started my academic career that I owed him a debt to teach black literature in a certain way. "Less time needs to be spent on the dragons," as he told me once, "and more on our ability to forge swords for battle, and the skill with which we've used them."

The man at the Christmas party, of course, would rather that I talk about the dragons. And at first, when students take my class, they are surprised, even a bit disappointed, to see the course will not head in that direction. But by the end of the semester, they have been invariably uplifted by the heroic nature of African Americans, in part, perhaps, because it is the nature found in us all.

BULLETS

*T*he pharmacist was an elderly black man whose hands trembled as much as mine. I watched the paper flutter as he held it close to his face, trying to read my writing, which was all but illegible in the true fashion of doctors. But I wasn't a doctor. I was just a twenty-year-old unit clerk who forged prescriptions.

I often wrote them for barbiturates but I liked amphetamines most. They mimicked the high I got from cocaine and they were easier to consume; sometimes while at work, without missing a beat from the patients' labs I was filing, I'd just toss a few in my mouth and chew them like cashews. I couldn't do that with cocaine. And besides, cocaine was expensive and lasted only a few hours, whereas a bottle of Dexedrine was relatively cheap and could last a week or more, depending, of course, on how many I prescribed.

This was a felony, I understood, punishable by many years in prison, so I tried to take the right precautions. I knew to use the doctors' narcotics numbers I stole only once, and I never revisited the same pharmacy. I knew, too, that it was important to look like a respectable member of society, so I always wore a suit and tie and sometimes I carried *The Wall Street Journal*. But these things cannot help you when your nose, raw from cocaine use, suddenly begins to bleed.

The pharmacist had left by then to fill my order. He was thirty feet away, standing behind a glass partition and looking at rows of shelves crammed with colorful bottles, when a gush of liquid rushed over my lips and down my chin. This would be a bad one, I knew, as these kinds of bleeds often were, as persistent and messy as a gunshot to the temple. While I dug in my pocket for the tissue that I always carried for such an occasion, I tilted my head back, trying to keep the blood where it belonged, but all that did was redirect its descent so that now it trailed down both of my cheeks. I tore off two small pieces of Kleenex and stuffed them in each nostril, and then I used the rest of it to begin wiping my face and neck. Unfortunately, the pharmacist came back before I could finish.

"*Good Lord,* young man, are you all right?"

I put the bloody tissue in my jacket pocket and lowered my gaze from the ceiling to the old man, who was removing his glasses and looking very concerned. The thing to do here was run, but I had enough coke and alcohol in my system to make me think I could talk my way out of this. Especially when I saw that he was holding the white bag containing my Dexedrine. I leaned against the counter, hoping I looked casual, like some guy in a bar waiting for his martini, except that my nostrils were clogged with paper and my face was smeared with blood. I opened my mouth to offer an explanation, but I'd lost my nerve. All that came out was, "I'll be okay."

The pharmacist nodded slowly, a gesture of sudden understanding. "Can I see some identification, Mr. . . ."—he put his glasses on and lifted the bag to his face—"Mr. Jenkins?"

I patted my pockets, then pointed toward the door and said my wallet was in the car. As I backed away, he stood there not moving, waiting for me to step outside, perhaps, so he could reach for the phone to call the police. But if he intended to do so, I'd be long gone by the time they arrived, and all they'd find would be two pieces of tissue, small and bloodied, like bullets taken from a corpse.

THE MECHANICS OF BEING

*W*hen I'd decided to write a novel based on my life I was in the Iowa Writers' Workshop, starting my second year. I'd recently found some statistics that said there'd been a 60 percent chance I'd end up dead or in jail; I had stories to prove just how close I'd come. But after writing the first draft, my tale of black teenage delinquency seemed too clichéd to me, told too often before. I decided to write about my father instead.

My father lost his sight when he was twelve. Climbing the stairs to his Chicago brownstone, he somehow fell backward, hitting his head hard against the pavement and filling his cranium with blood. It would have been better had some of this blood seeped out, alerting him to seek medical attention, but when the area of impact did no more than swell a little and throb, he tended himself by applying two cubes of ice and eating six peanut butter cookies. He did not tell anyone about the injury. He also did not mention the two weeks of headaches that followed, the month of dizzy spells, or that the world was growing increasingly, terrifyingly dim.

His mother had died of cancer four years earlier. His alcoholic father was rarely around. So at home my father only had to conceal his condition from his grandmother, Mama Alice, who herself could barely see past her cataracts, and his three older brothers and sister, who had historically paid him little attention. His grades at school suffered, but his teachers believed him when he said his discovery of girls was the cause. He spent less and less time with his friends, gave up baseball altogether, and took to walking with the aid of a tree branch. In this way his weakening vision remained undetected for three months until, one morning at breakfast, things fell apart.

Mama Alice greeted him as he sat at the table. She was by the stove, he knew, from the location of her voice. As he listened to her approach, he averted his face. She put a plate in front of him and another to his right, where she always sat. She pulled a chair beneath her. He reached for his fork, accidentally knocking it off the table. When several seconds had passed and he'd made no move, Mama Alice reminded him that forks couldn't fly. He took a deep breath and reached down to his left, knowing that to find the utensil would be a stroke of good fortune, since he couldn't even see the floor. After a few seconds of sweeping his fingers against the cool hardwood, he sat back up. There was fear in Mama Alice's voice when she asked him what was wrong. There was fear in his when he confessed he couldn't see.

He confessed everything then, eager, like a serial killer at last confronted with evidence of his crime, to have the details of his awful secret revealed. And when pressed about why he hadn't said anything sooner, he mentioned his master plan: He would make his sight get better by ignoring, as much as possible, the fact that it was getting worse.

For gutting out his fading vision in silence, Mama Alice called him brave. His father called him a fool. His teachers called him a liar. His astonished friends and siblings called him Merlin. The doctors called him lucky. The damage was reversible, they said, because the clots that had formed on and now pressed against his occipital lobes could be removed. But they were wrong; those calcified pools of blood were in precarious locations and could not be excised without risking immediate paralysis or worse. The surgeons inserted a metal plate (my father never knew why) and later told Mama Alice that the clots would continue to grow, not only destroying the little sight he had left but also killing him. They gave him one more year to live, but they were wrong again.

They were wrong, too, in not predicting the seizures. He'd have them the rest of his life, internal earthquakes that toppled his body and pitched it violently across the floor. I remember these scenes vividly: As a young child, I would cower with my siblings at a safe distance while my mother, her body clamped on top of my father's, tried to put medicine in his mouth before he chewed off his tongue. My father was a big man in those days, bloated on fried food and Schlitz—one wrong move of his massive body would have caused my mother great harm—but she rode him expertly, desperately, a crocodile hunter on the back of her prey.

I always expected one of those attacks to be fatal. But their damage would be done over five decades rather than all at once, slowly and insidiously eroding his brain, like water over stone. So we knew it wasn't Alzheimer's when he began forgetting the people and things that mattered and remembering the trivia of his youth. He knew it, too. That's why, at the age of fifty-five, he retired from teaching, moved with my mother to an apartment in the suburbs, and waited, like we all waited, for the rest of his mind to wash away. By the time I began teaching, when he was in his midsixties, he had forgotten us all.

According to the American Foundation for the Blind, every seven minutes someone in this country will become blind or visually impaired. There are 1.3 million blind people in the United States. Less than half of the blind complete high school, and only 30 percent of working-age blind adults are employed. For African Americans, who make up nearly 20 percent of this population, despite being only 12 percent of the population at large, the statistics are even bleaker.

There are no reliable statistics for the number of unemployed blind prior to the 1960s, but some estimates put it as high as 95 percent. Most parents of blind children then had low expectations, hoping only that they would find some more useful role to play in society than selling pencils on street corners or playing a harmonica in some subway station, accompanied by a bored though faithful basset hound. Usually the blind were simply kept at home.

Mama Alice expected to keep my father at home for just a year, but even that was one year too many. She was elderly, diabetic, arthritic, and still mourning for her daughter and other accumulated losses. Now she had to care for a blind boy who spent his days crying or, when his spirits lifted, smashing things in his room. His school had expelled him, his friends had fled, and his sister and brothers had not been moved by his handicap to develop an interest in his affairs. And so on the second anniversary of his predicted death, Mama Alice packed up his things, kissed him good-bye, implored him to summon more bravery, and sent him to jail.

My father never told any of his children about this. I read about it in his chart at the Sight Saving School, in Jacksonville, Illinois, where he'd been transferred after fifteen months in juvenile detention. In 1994, the same year he and my mother moved to the suburbs, Brenda and I paid a visit to that school.

Sixteen years later the trip for me is a blur, punctuated now and then with random vivid images. I cannot see the face of the principal who greeted us, and I cannot visualize the office we were escorted to, but my father's chart is seared in my mind, a black three-ring binder with THOMAS KELLER WALKER handwritten on the top right corner. Before I read it, the principal gave us a tour of the facilities. It was an enormous complex that included basketball courts, a baseball diamond, a swimming pool . . . and classrooms. We were taken to the library, which was a museum of sorts, where the history of blindness was laid out in pictures and graphs behind glass cases. We ate lunch in the cafeteria where my father had eaten lunch. We went to the dorm room where he'd slept. Outside, we walked on the track where, cane in hand, my father learned to run again.

After the tour, the principal took us back to her office and left us alone with his chart. It contained his height, weight, vital signs, and a summary of his academic performance before he lost his sight, which I cannot recall, though my guess is that it was exceptional. I also cannot remember the progress reports during his two years there. What I do remember is a description of him as "traumatized." That seemed about right to me. He'd lost his mother, his sight, and his freedom. The only person who'd consistently showed him love had put him in prison. He was sixteen. I thought about my own life at sixteen, my delinquency and lack of purpose, and I suddenly felt as disappointed in myself as I know he must have been.

When we arrived back at our home in Iowa City, I typed up my notes from the trip. I decided not to call my father to ask about being put in juvenile detention; he'd had a reason for keeping it a secret, and I figured I should probably honor it.

In 1997 my parents moved again. My father was having difficulty with his balance and could not manage the stairs to their second-floor apartment. They bought a house in Dolton, a suburb south of Chicago; its primary appeal, besides being a single-level ranch, was its screened-in porch. For two summers they pretty much lived in that porch, crowding it with a swing set, a glider, a card table, on which sat an electric water fountain, and four reclining chairs. My father was in one of those chairs enjoying a refreshing breeze and the faint sound of gurgling water when he had a grand mal seizure, the worst in years. For two weeks he was in intensive care on a respirator. When he was finally able to breathe on his own, he was moved to a regular room, and a month later, when he could finally speak, he asked everyone, including my mother, his wife of forty-two years, who they were. While he languished in this state of oblivion, struggling to recall his life, I finished the first draft of my book, having him die peacefully in his sleep. Wishful thinking. Another massive seizure put him back in the ICU.

A month later he was transferred to an assisted living facility. Speech therapists helped him talk again, and occupational therapists showed him how to move with a walker. But no one could fix his brain. His thoughts were in a thousand fragments, floating in his skull, I imagined, like the flakes of a shaken snow globe. His filter gone, my father, this intensely private man, from whom I'd had difficulty extracting just the basic facts of his life, was now a mental flasher. My mother called me on occasion to report what he'd revealed.

"Mama Alice arrested me," he announced to her one day.

"I drink too much," he said on another.

"That Lynne can sure fry some chicken," he mentioned as well. After my mother relayed this last comment, there was a long pause before she asked me, "You *do* know about Lynne, don't you?"

Lynne was the woman he'd left her for. That was in 1963, thirteen years after my parents had met at the Chicago Lighthouse for the Blind, an organization that, among other services, provides employment for the visually impaired. My father was there assembling clocks while home on summer break from the Sight Saving School, and my mother had been hired to do the same. They were seventeen when they met, eighteen when they married, and at twenty-five the parents of four children. My mother was pregnant with me and my twin when my father moved out. That was all I knew, told to me one day by my brother Tim when I was in my midteens.

My parents had never discussed any of this with my siblings or me. My mother spoke openly about it now, though, and then she segued into talking about the man she'd dated during the two-year separation and about the son they'd had together. Her story I knew more about because when my twin and I were ten or so, her son, our half brother, would come to our house to play with us. Occasionally he'd be accompanied by his father, a lanky blind man who chain-smoked and had a baritone voice that made me think of God. These attempts at civility lasted two summers before suddenly coming to an end. I never again saw my mother's son. And I never met my father's. I had not even known that he and Lynne had one, in fact, until three years ago, when my brother Tommy mailed me a newspaper clipping from the *Chicago Sun-Times* detailing his murder. His girlfriend had stabbed him thirty-one times. In the margins, next to his picture, Tommy had inscribed, "He looks just like *you!*" At first glance, I had thought it was.

I made no mention of my half brothers in the novel, nor did I write about my parents' separation, even though my mother, after speaking about this tumultuous period in their lives and of the resilient love that saw her and my father through it, suggested that I should. But at the time these details seemed peripheral to my point, too far astray from the topic at hand, not so much character development and depth, in my view, as dirty laundry. After chronicling how he'd lost his sight, I'd described how my father had navigated the sighted world: his learning to walk with a cane, his mastery of public transportation, how he'd earned his college degrees with the help of student and technological aides, his purchase of a Seeing Eye dog. Chapter after chapter focused on the mechanics of blindness when I should have focused on the mechanics of being. I should have explored my father's life beyond his handicap, just as, when I set out to write my own story, I should have explored my life beyond the trials common to inner-city black males. The unpublished novels I had written said no more about the range of my father's experiences or mine, no more about the meanings we had shaped from the chaos of our lives, than the newspaper clipping had said about his murdered son's.

I realized this while at my father's funeral. He died in September 2005, fifty-six years after the surgeons predicted he would, succumbing not to the blood clots after all, but rather to pneumonia. Brenda and I left Dorian and Adrian with her mother and flew to Chicago to attend the service. We sat in the second pew, just behind my mother, whose shoulder I would reach forward to pat as we listened to the organist play my father's favorite hymns. A cousin of mine read scriptures, a family friend recited a number of poems, and then the pastor gave the eulogy, a thorough account of my father's accomplishments punctuated by the refrain: *and he did this while blind.* It was while I listened to him try to convince us that sightlessness was the core and sum of my father's existence that I understood why my novels had failed.

At some point during the eulogy, when I could no longer stand to listen, an incident I had long forgotten came to mind. I was probably thirteen years old, and my father, as he had so often before, asked me to take some of his clothes to the dry cleaner. Ordinarily this wasn't a big deal, but I had plans to join some friends at the park, so I whined and complained about being called into service. A mild argument ensued, which I lost, and a short while later I stormed out of the house with a paper bag full of his things. At the cleaners, I watched the clerk remove each article of clothing, my boredom turning to horror as her hand, now frozen midair, dangled before us a pair of my father's boxers. The clerk, very pretty and not much older than me, smiled and said, "We don't clean *these.*" I couldn't believe that my father had made such an unpardonable mistake, a blunder of the highest order, and the more I thought of it the more upset I became. Halfway home, swollen with anger and eager to release it, I started to run. When I arrived, out of breath, my hands clenched by my sides, my father wasn't in the living room, where I'd left him, but sitting on the porch. The second I barked, *"Daddy!"* he exploded in laughter, his large stomach quivering beneath his T-shirt, his ruddy face pitched toward the sky. I could not, despite my best effort, help but join him.

I rose after the pastor finished his eulogy and told this story to the congregation. If I ever attempt to write another novel about my father, this is where it will begin.

WHEN LOVE SPEAKS

I wasn't homeless, per se; it's just that none of the homes was mine. They belonged to various girlfriends, some of whom are as blurred to me now as the substances I abused. Most of these women were substance abusers themselves, though some were merely depressed or afflicted with self-esteem so low that having me stay with them, even for brief periods, struck them as a good idea. I did not love these women, it is fair to say, and it is fair to say that they did not love me.

I knew very little about love in those days. But I knew a great deal about hatred, and most of what I experienced was my own hatred of me. That's how I ended up with Pam. She was aggressive, rude, domineering, and deceitful, traits that even in my confused state I did not care for, and yet I stayed with her for two long years, following her from apartment to apartment whenever she got the urge to move.

There were separations during those periods, times when one of our frequent fights sent me cramming my worldly possessions into a duffel bag and sleeping at a former girlfriend's house or, if it was warm, in my car, a fifteen-year-old Lincoln Continental so large that the backseat was in essence a small bed. But invariably I'd end up back at Pam's door, admission guaranteed, I knew, if I returned with coke in hand.

After one of those departures, which lasted only three hours, since I could find no one to let me stay with her, and since it was winter, I returned to Pam's apartment just as a man was leaving. I watched him from the end of the hall as he walked a few feet away, removed a key from his pocket, and entered another unit. A moment later I found Pam in our bedroom, her nude body floating along the waves of her waterbed, her left hand holding a cigarette. When she heard the floorboard squeak beneath my feet, she slowly turned in my direction. "I hope you brought some coke," she said. It occurred to me, then, that I needed a home of my own.

But that was easier said than done; I'd filed for bankruptcy two years earlier when I was nineteen, so I knew the odds of someone granting me a lease were slim. This was proved true over the next several months. I was rejected by every place I applied, often right on the spot, forcing me to remain at Pam's apartment, where I slept on the couch with her three mangy cats. Her "boyfriend" visited her openly now, occasionally letting himself in with his own key. I would leave, then, sometimes driving to the medical center to sleep in the parking garage until my shift began.

Oddly enough, Pam and I got along better then than ever, our contempt for each other morphing into something that resembled, if not friendship, then a truce between combatants. When my car finally died of complications associated with old age, it was she who drove me to the apartments to fill out applications. It was because of her, in fact, that I got my first place.

It was in a high-rise on the Near South Side, right in the thick of a ghetto, with housing projects as far as the eye could see, though the complex itself was decidedly upscale. The lawns were nicely maintained, there was a swimming pool and tennis courts, and the views of the city were worthy of some posh hotel. The property had been recently constructed, a part of an attempt to revitalize the area. Surely, a guy in bankruptcy wasn't the kind of tenant they sought. The building manager, a matronly black woman with steel-gray hair, told me that in so many words while

Pam and I sat in her office. My credit report was in the manager's hand, and as she delivered the bad news, I noticed that she kept sneaking glances at Pam and shaking her head.

"I don't know what that old bitch's problem was," Pam said as we drove back to her apartment. "Did you see those looks she kept giving me?"

"Yeah," I said. "I definitely picked up a bad vibe."

"*Bitch,*" Pam spat. "I'm glad you didn't get that place. No need to be giving that hussy your money."

I agreed, just for the sake of being agreeable, and then I put the manager out of my mind, until she called me the next day at work and asked me to come see her alone.

When I arrived, I saw that my credit report was still on her desk. "I'm going to talk to you now," she began as I took a seat, "not as a building manager would to a client, but as a mother would to a son. First, I want you to tell me how old you are?"

"Twenty-one."

"And your lady friend?"

"Thirty."

She shook her head. "You have no business with that woman. She's no good; I know that like I know my own name. Just looking at you sitting there with her yesterday nearly broke my heart. You're a good person—I can sense that. I know you've made some mistakes; taking up with that woman was one of them. But the fact that you're trying to get away from her is a sign that you're aiming to do better, and I don't want to go to my grave thinking I could have helped you and I didn't. So I'm going to take a chance on you, son. I'm going to take a gamble. Now you have an opportunity to start over. Make good use of it. Don't let me down. Now, come on," she said, breaking into a smile as she rose from her chair. "Let's go take a look at your new home."

And even I, who knew so little about love in those days, knew all there was to know about it then.

TWO BOYS

*T*he two boys were in the backseat screaming for their mother, who was behind them in the parking lot, dying of a bullet wound to the thigh. The fact that Steve had shot her in a leg allowed me to hope that he wasn't trying to kill her, but his lawyers would not make that argument during his trial. They would simply portray him as a victim, a person who should be pitied and prayed for, as if he, like the two boys, had also been strapped in a booster seat, speeding from a mall with a killer.

He let them out just before pulling onto 79th Street. They ran back to their mother, not comprehending her nonresponsiveness because they were only five and six. They would not be called to testify.

Katrina, Steve's accomplice, would be. While he performed the jacking, she'd sat in an adjacent car, also stolen, watching with horror as a long prison sentence played out before her. Her lawyers would ask the jury for pity too. They'd explain how Steve, without telling Katrina his intentions, had driven with her to the mall, parked, told her to get in the driver's seat, and then approached a blue Intrepid, pointed his gun at the driver, and ordered her to get out. The twenty-eight-year-old victim whirled and lunged for her sons. Steve fired through the window. When Katrina was asked why she didn't flee, she would testify that she was too afraid, citing Steve's history of physical and mental abuse. Just the night before, he'd beaten her and then locked her in their bedroom while he went to find them more dope. She saw no choice, she'd tell the jury, but to follow him, just as he'd commanded her to.

They headed east, weaving recklessly through the two-lane traffic. I would read this part of the court transcript and remember Steve's love of drag racing, how he'd challenge any drivers who were teenagers like us. The challenge taken, we'd hit speeds of sixty or more where the limit was only thirty, plowing through stop signs and red lights, seeking, it seems in hindsight, evidence that we were mortal. We didn't find it then, but the proof is surely upon us now, as my hair has thinned and grayed, and Steve sits on death row.

The crime occurred in March 2001. My twin brother saw the story on the evening news. When he called to tell me, I remember being grateful that I no longer lived in the kind of place that produces junkies who shoot mothers. Chicago's South Side is a factory for such people, rolling them out like so many assembly-line toys, each seemingly no different from the other. That apparent lack of distinction would be why, during the trial, Steve's court-appointed lawyers would offer the same tired excuses: a life of poverty, an abusive father, a neglectful mother, the tormenting want of love and attention. And that is also why the jury would turn a deaf ear on this defense, and on Katrina's too.

I did not know Katrina. By the time Steve committed this murder—his *second*—I did not know him; the last time I'd seen him was in 1984. My girlfriend Pam and I had just scored some coke and stopped at a liquor store when Steve swaggered from the shadows. A woman clung to his arm. I invited them back to my apartment to get high. Steve and I had lost touch for many years because he was in and out of jail, and while it was good to see him again, it was also uncomfortable. I had already begun to doubt my commitment to the thug life, whereas he seemed to be embracing it tighter, wedding himself to a brazen lawlessness that frightened me. Proof of this came late in the night, long after we'd all turned in. Pam and I were in our bed, while Steve and his friend were in the living room on the couch, both asleep, it seemed, as I passed them on my way to the bathroom. But when I returned a moment later, Steve was gone. And then I heard Pam scream. I ran into my room just as he scrambled off the bed, his boxers bunched at his heels. It was the kind of foolhardy act for which men have lost their lives, and yet at that moment I felt, for some reason, that *my* life was the one in danger. My voice trembling less from outrage than fear, I told him to leave. He went to the couch and woke his female companion, yelling at her as though the whole thing had been her fault. As she dressed, she cast me a quick glance; perhaps remembering the hopelessness in her eyes is why I cannot help but feel sympathy for Katrina, even though I did not know her, and even though her version of events may not be true.

"I didn't know he had a gun," she would testify, insisting that she thought they were at the mall only to shoplift. I believe that. I believe, too, her claim to have deliberately caused an accident in order to attract police. A young man whose pregnant wife was in the passenger seat was driving the car she rear-ended. The man got out to inspect the damage, and then he went to confront Katrina. Steve pulled beside them and told her to drive away. She did. Steve did too. The man ran back to his car and gave chase. When he caught up to Katrina and began yelling profanities through his window, Steve shot at him twice. The man took off, heading west. Steve and Katrina, still in their separate cars, went east.

Steve wanted to find a chop shop. Katrina had said she knew where one was on the West Side. They made several stops along the way—a liquor store, a gas station, Katrina's mother's house, her sister's, closer and closer to a place that did not exist; Katrina had made up the whole thing, simply trying to buy more time. When it seemed to be running out, she caused another crash, this time hitting two parked cars, the impact with the second being so violent that her car flipped and threw her to the curb. Witnesses descended from all directions. One of them had called for an ambulance before telling her help was on the way. Steve, pretending to be just another concerned witness, pushed through the crowd and said he'd help her right now. He asked for and received directions to the nearest hospital, and then he picked up Katrina and put her in the Intrepid. As they drove away, he pressed the gun to her temple. It's difficult for me to imagine that, by then, a part of her didn't want him to pull the trigger. When the police captured them a short while later, I suspect it was one of the happiest moments of her life.

Five years after their arrest, Steve was among the ranks of condemned inmates, while I was among the ranks of college faculty, toying with the idea of going to see him. I'd reviewed the visitation rules and regulations. I'd even priced tickets from Boston to Chicago. I had imagined us sitting across from each other, separated by three inches of Plexiglas, both of us holding phones. I knew we'd start the hour by recollecting the better times of our youth, how we'd made out with girls in his brother's immobile Mustang, or the dance moves we'd rehearse before going to house parties. We'd mention the first times we got high, and then our forays into petty crimes, the botched ones making us shake our heads and smile. "Remember that time," he would probably say, "when I teased you for wanting to take those groceries back to that old lady?" When we erupted in laughter, the other inmates and visitors would look our way, wondering what could be so funny, and Steve and I would know that, behind this lighthearted veneer, nothing actually was. He was going to be executed, and I was not, even though we were both assembly-line toys, manufactured with parts that weren't intended to last. Mine had—he'd hate me for that. But I'd hate him too. Because for the entire visit, I'd be thinking about *my* two boys, aged four and six, and imagining them in a world, for no good reason, without a mother.

PRINCIPLES OF MATH

When my shift ended at midnight, I stopped at a liquor store and picked up a six-pack and a quart of gin. As soon as I entered my apartment I put the beer in the freezer because I liked it best when it had a certain chill. It was ready by the time I had finished eating a can of chili and half a dozen Ritz. I didn't have a coffee table, so I sprinkled some of my coke on a plate and then sat in front of my window. I lived on the sixteenth floor with a nice view of the city, including the Sears Tower, and when I looked to the right I could see the Illinois Central Railroad that carried executives downtown to make the kind of money I figured I'd never see.

I snorted a line every fifteen minutes or so until a quarter of the coke was gone. I needed to take it easy, though, because the coke had to last me at least three days. After a couple more lines, I told myself to stop.

By 3:00 AM I was licking the empty package, fiendish for more.

I paged Stan six times but he didn't answer, so I started drinking gin and tonics, trying to bring myself down quickly, hoping to avoid the depression of a dwindling coke high. But somewhere between my seventh and tenth drinks I got very depressed. And as usual, when I got very depressed, I wanted to talk to someone, anyone, about anything—politics, college, anything at all. I finished another drink and got my coat. The rest of that night comes back to me in flashes, as if there were a giant strobe light in the sky.

I'm jogging in a park . . . vomiting at the base of a tree . . . lying in a field of frost-covered grass . . . fleeing from the growl of an unseen dog . . . ducking when I hear sporadic gunfire . . . walking faster at the sound of footsteps . . . running when angry voices call . . . and now I'm only a few blocks from my apartment, standing before a cluster of buildings that I know belong to the Illinois Institute of Technology, the place where I'd once listened to math lectures with Tim.

And every time I think back to that night I'm overwhelmed by the belief that some cruel principle of math was at work, that some terrible law or theorem had determined, the instant I decided to let Tim school me, that standing there, at that exact moment, in that hopeless condition, was where I'd be.

OUTLAWS

*H*e appeared to have passed out, just another of the area's drunks or addicts; perhaps that's what the officer who first arrived on the scene believed. After approaching the idling car, which was blocking the intersection, he paused on the driver's side and tapped on the window. Inside, Tim was slumped against the door, his heart swollen and still.

"Cardiac arrest," my mother announced quietly when she called with the news. "That's what the doctors think, but we'll see." An autopsy was scheduled, which I assumed would point to drugs, even though by some accounts Tim had been clean of the hard stuff for years. But there'd been an epidemic of overdoses lately on Chicago's South Side, caused by one of those pure batches of heroin that sweeps through ghettos every now and then and carries scores of users to the morgue, a form of junkie population control. "We'll just have to wait and see," she said once more.

My sister Linda did not have to wait and see. "That *woman* poisoned him," she said when I phoned her. She was referring to Tim's wife. "That woman wanted his money." I noted that Tim had not had any money, not for a long while. "Oh, he *had* some money," she insisted. "And now she's going to try to get it."

"We'll have to stop her," I said.

"*Yes we will* have to stop her." She recalled all the serious troubles Tim had had with his wife during their few years together, which told me two things: Linda's intense hatred of Tim's wife was proving therapeutic, a temporary distraction from her grief, and her admiration of our brother had not waned, not even after he'd left school and become a hustler. In her mind's eye, she still saw him as a successful accountant, strutting down our street in his tailor-made suits and alligator shoes, or holding court on our front porch with teenaged boys who idolized him and sought to mimic his ways. I, of course, was one of those boys. And so was Jimmy. I called him next.

"Did you hear?" I asked. Jimmy said that he had. He fell silent, then, which wasn't unusual for him, because he wasn't much of a talker; whenever we called each other our conversations would be punctuated with long periods of awkward silence. But this time the silence wasn't awkward.

Finally, he said, "That woman poisoned him."

"She didn't poison him."

"How do you know?"

"I just know."

"Don't be so sure," he said. "Healthy forty-seven-year-olds don't just *drop dead* out of the blue."

Tim had not been healthy. When I'd seen him a year earlier, at our parents' fiftieth wedding anniversary party, he'd looked like he was dying, and maybe like he was aware of it. His face was ashen and swollen, his body gaunt, and his eyes recessed, blank, and frightened. His hair was mostly gray and patchy. After we'd shaken hands, I'd given him some of my discarded clothes, as had become my custom over the years, and watched as he riffled through the bag. He removed a pair of winter boots I'd never actually liked or worn, bought impulsively, like much of my wardrobe, after some wild victory or defeat. Without expression he slipped off his shoes, a pair of brown loafers that I'd given him too, put on the boots, and then took a few trial steps, looking down admiringly as he moved in small circles through the weedy grass. Around us, dozens of relatives and friends milled about my parents' backyard or sat at one of the card tables playing bid whist. Bottles and cups of liquor were plentiful; the summer air charged with pot and gangsta rap. Tim now stood before me, searching through the bag again, examining each item that I'd returned with from a larger world he'd elected not to see. Looking up, he asked, "Got a few bucks?"

I had twenty-five dollars for him in my front pocket, but there was a ritual to be followed. "Nope," I said.

He grinned. "Now how does a big-time *college professor* not have no money."

"Shit, *man,* times is *hard,*" I replied, slipping easily into the dialect of my youth.

"*Come on,* Jerry," Tim persisted. "Just a few bucks."

I protested once more before relenting. He stuffed the bills into his pocket, told me he'd catch me later, and then, leaving his loafers behind, like the remnants of an abduction, headed toward the car in which he would die.

I went to find Brenda. She was in the living room on the couch, our three-year-old son Dorian asleep in her arms, despite the dozen friends and relatives chatting nearby. Brenda looked at me quizzically and asked, "Where's Adrian?" As if on cue, our five-year-old walked into the room with a few of his young cousins, drinking a beer. Brenda leapt to her feet as I lunged at him, snatching away the can before sweeping him into my arms. One of my nephews tried to put us at ease, explaining that Adrian had not had very much. He and the others turned and ran outside.

Brenda's usually quiet voice was loud enough to carry through the room when she announced it was time to go. Some of the males glanced our way, snickering.

"Time to *go?*" I responded, facing not her but the growing gallery. "*Time to go?* Hell you talking about, woman? *I* decides when it's time to go."

"*Drop* it," she told me.

We said our good-byes.

The next two times I saw Tim were at funerals, the first one our father's, the second one his. He looked better the second time. So much better, in fact, that I didn't recognize him. Neither did Linda, who reached the coffin a step before me, staggered backward, and then turned and said, "That's not him!" I moved around her and looked. She was right. The man lying there was definitely not our brother. There was a vague resemblance, as if they might have been distant relatives, but something I could not pinpoint was off. The calmness of his expression? The waxy smoothness of his skin? I didn't know. But whoever this person was, he had freakishly large hands that I sensed were about to grab me. I staggered backward, too. I searched for and found an employee and told him of their shameful mistake. But he assured me that the mistake was mine. "That *is* Timothy Walker," he said.

My mother, Linda, and I, the first of our family to arrive, sat in the front pew. A moment later Jimmy sat behind us with his kids, and then my sister Mary arrived with her family, followed by my brother Tommy and his. Twenty minutes passed before our youngest sibling, André, entered the room moving very slowly down the aisle with an IV pole. A "johnny" hung beneath his unbuttoned blazer. He'd come directly from the hospital, where he'd lived for several weeks after being riddled with a rival gang's bullets. This was the second time he'd been shot. I figured we'd bury him next, though sometimes I wasn't so sure because Jimmy's life was hard. He was a single father of three, working as an orderly while also taking classes at a community college in hopes of a more meaningful career. Sitting next to me in the pew, he looked unhealthy and exhausted, just as Tim had when I saw him last.

Tommy, by contrast, could have been a model for *GQ*. He was a vice president of a large bank, and he and his wife of twenty-seven years had raised their three children with unflinching discipline and

far from the enticements of a ghetto. Their oldest child was studying at MIT, the second-born was at Northwestern, and the
youngest was headed for the Oberlin Conservatory. It had been
clear to me for some time that my life would have taken a very different course had I modeled myself after Tommy, and even
though I knew he was keenly aware of this fact, he never told me
so. But one day I would tell it to him. I respect the choices you
made with your life, I would say, and I would say the same thing
to Linda, a financial investor, and to Mary, a high school music
teacher. But as I glanced at their grief-stricken faces, I knew that
this was not the time or place.

The eulogy for Tim was fitting in that it didn't resemble the
brother I'd come to know any more than the body before us did.
Maybe since I'd last seen him he'd become a family man, religious
and law-abiding, a model citizen in all ways. It certainly was possible, because that was what he was in his youth. I think back to
those days sometimes and see him poring over his Bible, memo-
rizing the scriptures that he'd recite when we'd gathered for dinner. I see him helping Linda and Mary with their homework or
relieving our mother of washing the dishes. I see him playing
catch with Tommy, teaching André how to walk, and showing
Jimmy and me how to shoot pool. I see him typing letters for our
father. We all loved Tim. He was thoughtful and kind, the embodiment of virtue, much as the minister was describing him
now.

The eulogy ended. One by one, mourners began to rise and
offer testimony to Tim's life, including our childhood friends
Paul, Rob, and Louis. Next, the minister asked if any members of
the immediate family would like to say a few words. Maybe because I had done so at our father's funeral, my brothers and sisters
looked at me. But I, like them, was grief-stricken; I couldn't speak
at that moment. I shook my head no. The minister cued the organist and she began to play. A line of people, starting with the

pews in the rear, approached the casket to view Tim's body. When it was my turn to go, I declined. I feared that if I did, the vision of his strange-looking corpse would haunt me. So far it hasn't.

This is the vision that has: Tim is sitting next to me on our living room couch. We are high, and he is schooling me. He abruptly stops talking and focuses on the television, where the notorious Clyde Barrow emerges from a Model B Ford, parked along a quiet country road. The camera pans a few feet away to a patch of shrubs and trees, which suddenly rustle, causing birds to burst from their nests seconds before the air fills with the gunfire of six concealed officers. The first shot hits Clyde in the shoulder, twisting his body full-circle before throwing it to the ground, and then the other bullets come, ripping into his flesh while his companion, Bonnie Parker, still sitting in the car, opens her mouth to scream, and the bullets find her too. By the time the silence resumes, the couple lie in motionless, ravaged heaps. I glance at Tim. He is staring at the young outlaws, his face frozen in rapt concentration, his head bobbing slowly, and I will always wonder if he was calculating the odds of his own premature death, weighing the mathematical probabilities of getting rich off the streets versus his life ending too soon.

And it did end too soon. But there were no riches. There was no notoriety. There wasn't even any gunfire. All he got was a single officer, tapping on the window of his car.

EPILOGUE: CLOWNS

A man holding a fistful of money waved us into a parking lot, where another man pointed to an empty space between two minivans. I sped into the designated area and slammed on the brakes. I was unbuckling my seat belt when Dorian retched again, as he had twice during our race to Boston. The poor boy suffered from motion sickness, but fortunately it was triggered only when we were late for something and I was forced to weave at high speeds through traffic. Before we'd left the house, I'd had the foresight to grab a plastic grocery bag; half of Dorian's face was buried in that now. Adrian sat looking at his little brother with heartbreaking concern, while Brenda sat looking at me with simmering anger. That was okay. All of this would be forgotten, I knew, once we got inside.

I hurried everyone from the car and we fell in with a stream of pedestrians, most of them children. After a quick glance at my watch I told Brenda we simply had to go faster. She hoisted Dorian into her arms, muttering something unpleasant as I reached for Adrian. She didn't return my weak attempt at a smile before we started to jog. We shaved probably a minute off our time, every second of it vital, I knew, and well worth the pain in my knees and lower spine.

"We made it," I said, once we'd entered the building and found our seats.

"We're even a little *early*," Brenda noted.

"You can't be *early* for the circus, can you boys?"

"No!" they said in unison. They were happy and excited, just as I knew they would be. And Dorian's color had returned. He and Adrian sat on the edges of their seats, staring, like the hundreds of people around us, toward the center ring, where at any moment the ringmaster would appear in a top hat perched upon, according to the program I'd just opened, an Afro. The blurb beneath his photo proudly proclaimed that he was the first African American to hold this position in the Ringling Brothers' glorious history. That was interesting, I suppose, but I really didn't care. I doubted anyone else did either.

The lights dimmed, triggering deafening, joyful shrieks. The auditorium filled with twirling dots of light from the handheld toys that were sold in the lobby. Dorian and Adrian twirled theirs. I twirled mine. Brenda looked at me and shook her head, though this time she returned my smile.

"*Ladies and gentlemen, children of all ages!*" a voice boomed through the darkness. I faced the center ring. A beam of light poured down as if from the heavens onto the ringmaster, who stood with his arms extended, moving his body in a slow circle to greet us all. "*Behold, the greatest show on earth!*" Clowns rushed in from all directions.

And there I sat with my wife and sons, once a juvenile delinquent and now a college professor, experiencing my first circus.

Behold indeed.

ACKNOWLEDGMENTS

I'd like to thank the James A. Michener Foundation for support early in my career, as well as the Iowa Writers' Workshop permanent faculty, James Alan McPherson, Marilynne Robinson, and the late Frank Conroy; its visiting faculty, Denis Johnson, Thom Jones, John Edgar Wideman, and Debra Eisenberg; and its staff, Connie Brothers and Deb West.

I am particularly grateful to Edward Homewood, for guiding me to the writer's life. Thank you to Gerald Gross, for plucking me out of the blue, and to my agent John "Ike" Taylor Williams, for introducing me to my wonderful editor, Beth Rashbaum.

For their careful readings of various drafts of this work, I'd like to thank Lois Poule, my wife, Brenda Molife, and my mother, Mary Walker. I also received valuable feedback on the manuscript from Robert Atwan, Mary Dondero, Courtney Smith, Jamie Nelson, and Shaylin Walsh.

For their encouragement and advice, I'd like to thank Mira Vujovic, Patricia Friend, Mercedes Nuñez, Roger Dunn, Tara Sullivan, James "Jake" Jakobsen, Mary O'Connell, Howard London, Anna Martin-Jerald, Alan Comedy, Lou Ricciardi, Dana Mohler-Faria, Aeon Skoble, and Tom Curley.

For their enthusiasm and inspiration, I'd like to thank my students at Bridgewater State College.

In addition to Harold Washington Community College (formerly "Loop"), I'd like to thank all community colleges for the invaluable opportunities they provide.

Thank you to my brothers and sisters, for the life we shared. Most important, I'd like to thank my parents, for their boundless love and support, and for their example of how to persevere.

I gratefully acknowledge the following magazines and anthologies in which some of these chapters appeared, sometimes in slightly different form: *The Iowa Review*, "Workshopped" and "Dragon Slayers" (under the single title "Dragon Slayers"); *The North American Review*, "Scattered Inconveniences"; *The Missouri Review*, "The Mechanics of Being"; *The New Delta Review*, "Captain Walker"; *The Chronicle of Higher Education*, "Visible Man" and "Game" (under the title "Teaching, and Learning, Racial Sensitivity"); *Brothers: 26 Stories of Love and Rivalry*, "Sacraments of Reconciliation"; *The Writer's Presence*, "Scattered Inconveniences"; *America Now*, "Game" (under the title "Teaching, and Learning, Racial Sensitivity"); *The Best African American Essays 2009*, "We Are Americans"; *The Literary Review*, "Two Boys."

"Workshopped" and "Dragon Slayers" also appeared in *The Best American Essays 2007* (under the single title "Dragon Slayers"), and "The Mechanics of Being" also appeared in *The Best American Essays 2009*.

ABOUT THE TYPE

This book was set in Garamond, a typeface originally designed by the Parisian typecutter Claude Garamond (1480–1561). This version of Garamond was modeled on a 1592 specimen sheet from the Egenolff-Berner foundry, which was produced from types assumed to have been brought to Frankfurt by the punchcutter Jacques Sabon.

Claude Garamond's distinguished romans and italics first appeared in *Opera Ciceronis* in 1543–44. The Garamond types are clear, open, and elegant.